HAPPY DAYS

and Dark Nights

Jerry and Susanne McClain

WITH MARSHA GALLARDO

WESTERN FRONT, LTD.,
PUBLISHING COMPANY

PALOS VERDES, CALIFORNIA

© 1996 Western Front Ltd., Publishing Company

ISBN 0-9641058-1-0

Western Front, Ltd.

Cover design: Karen Ryan, Palos Verdes, CA
Book design/typography: Publication Services, Redlands, CA
Printing: Griffin Printing, Glendale, CA
Manufactured in the United States of America

Dedication

We lovingly dedicate this book to…

Jarret Kent McClain

…our wonderful son who is always there with a smile, a hug and a prayer, and who has made us proud of him every day of his life.

May and Purl Horn (Mem and Pap)

…our precious grandparents whose dedication to the Lord and whose devotion to each other served as a lifetime example of real love and commitment.

B. Jerry McClain, Sr.

…my first hero and sports pal…and my dad

George and Helen Roshay
and
Don and Doris Charlesworth

…our parents, for nurturing our talents with all those music lessons, for their spiritual guidance, and for their love and support during the "Happy Days and Dark Nights."

Contents

Foreword

Who can forget Fonzie, Richie or any of the "Happy Days" TV gang — and how we all love to remember the lighthearted feeling that show's long run brought us. But my happiest "Happy Days" feeling relates to two people who were never on the show, but one of whom set our nation ringing with the "Happy Days" tune and lyrics.

I want you to get to know — and find real "Happy Days" with — Jerry and Susanne McClain!

Jerry is the singer of that classic theme song that still resonates around the world wherever "Happy Days" reruns continue to entertain televiewers. It has become a landmark melody in our culture, harking back not only to a fun TV show, but to a happier time in America's national life.

Jerry and Susanne's roles on stage as an artist and studio singer have put them center stage alongside some of the late 20th century's best known names. Professionally speaking, the McClains "have been around the barn and back" lots of times. Jerry's involvement in the whole entertainment scene is well known by friends and associates, and his contributions have been made in many ways. But still, the inescapable pulse beat of Jerry's "Happy Days" theme seems to overshadow everything else with its unforgettable and upbeat sentiment through the TV series. But enough of this public side of Jerry and Susanne McClain.

This book isn't about celebrities as much as it's about two human beings caught in a trap — and finally getting free. It's a statement of hope for everyone who finds that happy days have eluded them, and dark nights have overtaken them. Since that description applies at one time or another to about 95 percent of the people I've met or ministered to, it seems to me that the McClains' fascinating story and its glorious ending could mean a lot to you.

I want to say one more thing: the McClains are genuine-article people. I've been their pastor for quite a few years, and I can testify that they are people of solid stuff — with a genuine commitment to love God, care for people and serve their Savior in any way they can.

Let me recommend them — and their book. To know them through its pages will, I think, be a happy experience. But to discover the Truth in their story will do more than make you happy. HE can make you free!

—Jack W. Hayford
Senior Pastor, The Church On The Way
Van Nuys, California
December 1995

Foreword

From my earliest days as Campus Crusade for Christ Director at UCLA in the '60s, where I first met Jerry...to helping Susanne turn her life over to Jesus in my living room...to finally pronouncing them husband and wife...I knew God had something special for this gifted and vivacious couple.

We were close friends from the start. Over the next 30 years our paths crossed again and again, as they toured the country with their singing groups and I held prophecy crusades and lectures. I remember with deep appreciation the evening in Las Vegas when they were appearing with B.B. King, but took the time to drive across town to lead singing at the Convention Center where I was speaking. They brought their talent and integrity to both arenas.

It came as no surprise to me that their success led to the elite world of the entertainment business. But living in the "fast lane" of that world took its toll on the things that in the long run are most important in life.

In the midst of being "rich and famous," Jerry began to compromise and fell into drugs. He nearly lost all that was most precious to him — his walk with God, his wife, his son and his career.

This book is the true story of Jerry's restoration and Susanne's unfailing commitment to him. It reads like a modern-day enactment of the Biblical parable of the Prodigal Son. The amazing power of God's rescuing and restoring love will give every reader a sense of new hope, faith and assurance in these uncertain times. It will surely touch your heart and open up new dimensions of understanding about God's grace. You will see the power that a wife's love can have in some of the desperate circumstances so many married couples face because of the pressures of our generation.

This book is destined to encourage and challenge people in all walks of life — in all situations. I know you will receive a special blessing from reading it. I am personally thrilled to have had a part in the lives of my two dear friends Jerry and Susanne.

—Hal Lindsey

Preface

A little over 50 years ago, two people were born five days apart in Michigan and Oklahoma and grew up within 20 miles of each other in Van Nuys and Pasadena, California, with a love for singing and a destiny to serve God together.

One sang with her twin sister in the choir at the Catholic church and then signed a recording contract at age 16 and was a star on TV. The other sang on his dad's radio ministry for the Church of the Nazarene and was also on local television shows. Those voices later become one, and we are still singing together today.

On any given day, all over the world, our two voices enter homes singing "The Theme from Happy Days," while the well-known faces of The Fonz and Richie Cunningham flash on television screens.

"Happy Days" brought us a Gold Record and many music awards, plus a string of television appearances and nightclub engagements with top entertainers.

Tragically, Happy Days turned to Dark Nights when fame and fortune led to a devastating cocaine addiction, leaving our careers in shambles, our faith a distant memory, and our family crushed and in bankruptcy. Disobedience to God is heartbreaking, and our jagged path was not the Lord's choosing. But it was His choosing us that brought the pieces of our broken lives back together.

Our book, *Happy Days and Dark Nights*, is the

story of our American dream turned nightmare turned miracle. It's a "comeback story" of forgiveness, celebrating the power of God's redemptive and healing love.

We trust and pray that our story will reach hearts that are broken, and that it will bring hope and encouragement to the hopeless — because we were there ourselves. To those who dream of fame and fortune, we are living examples of the price you have to pay to reach that dream.

God has given us back all that we lost and more, and we will forever sing a new song and tell of His wondrous love.

—Jerry and Susanne McClain

Acknowledgments

With heartfelt thanks...

...to my twin sister, *Diane*, my best friend, who shared boyfriends, secrets, clothes, music lessons, dreams, joys and tears, and the stage with me all my life. And her husband, *Ed Finnegan*, who showed her that there was more to life than being on stage.

...to my brother, *Kent*, and wife, *Myrna*, who helped us keep family traditions and share summer vacations at Lake Almanore, even when we had no money.

...to my brother, *Dennis*, who had to play second fiddle to his twin sisters for so many years.

...to our dear prayer partners, *Larry and Sharon Griffith, Dick and Linda Sanner, Kurt and Patty Hardy, Glenn and Crystal McGinnis, Paul Johnson, Sandi Miller Denenburg, Carolyn Bushnell, Claudia Niesen* and family prayer warriors who stood by us with their love and support financially and prayerfully.

...to *Michael Omartian*, my friend for 30 years, my sports buddy and musical producer who gave us the opportunity to record *Happy Days*. And his wife, *Stormie*, who encouraged us to write this book.

...to *Pastor Jack Hayford*, for his leadership, prayer, and inspiring messages at Church On The Way, our home church for 25 years, and for graciously writing the foreword to our book.

…to *Min Whaley*, my counselor, whose healing words turned my bitterness and hatred for Jerry back into feelings of love, and who taught me the real meaning of "forgiveness."

…to *Hal Lindsey and Jan Lindsey* for playing such important roles in our lives over the last 30 years.

…to our good friends and musicians in The Lively Set — *Kenny Ballard, Terry Smith, Dave Fractman, Chuck Stokes, Jerry McCaskill* and *Pat Livingston* — who spent five years on stage with us entertaining audiences and ourselves.

…to our good friends and musicians in Brother Love — *Dave and Carmen Swanson, Bruce Lofgren, Zavier, Bill Hill, Lynn Coulter, "Barney" Robertson, Rod Schaub, Bob Walden* and *Dave Herring* — who helped us take the message of Jesus into all the corners of the earth; and to *Linda Pratt Best* and *Molly Coulter* for being Jarret's first nannies out on the road.

…to my singing partner and good friend, *Truett Pratt…* *"L.T.,"* who shared the stage with me during the "Happy Days" and many of the dark nights, and whose talent, warmth and charisma will be forever remembered and treasured.

…to *Steve Barri*, who co-produced "Happy Days" with Mike Omartian.

…to our personal managers, *Jim Fitzgerald, Alex Grob, Anita Kerr, Coffee Walker* and *Doug Lyon*, who believed in, nurtured and guided our talents.

...to dear friends *Dan Dalton, Jim and Debbie Roberson, Rob and Connie Palazzolo, Bill and Sue Goodale, Jeff Masters, Don Rugg, Lynda Minkler Romano, The Worldlie Sisters (Janet Pyle, Jan McGeary, Cecie Doucet, Debbie Yost and Barb Latt), the Borden family* (our great neighbors), *Bob Cotterell*, and the administration and teachers at Bishop Alemany High School and Village Christian School.

...to *Ken and Lori Ballard*, of The Ballard Company, for designing our press kit.

...to *Cliff Ford,* our publisher, who shares our vision and whose faith in us made this book a reality.

...to *Nikki Benjamin,* whose unending patience and attention to detail kept the book moving safely through the editing and production processes.

...to *Karen Ryan* for designing the cover of our book.

...to *Ron Widman* for the hours of editing and designing the interior of our book.

...and our very special thanks to co-author, *Marsha Gallardo,* who took all the pieces and events of our lives and wove them together into a musical tapestry. Her family is no doubt thanking God daily that this project is complete. We shall be forever grateful to her for helping us tell our story.

CHAPTER 1

Try to remember

BY HARRY SCHMIDT AND T. JONES

RECORDED BY THE LIVELY SET ON MERCURY RECORDS

Try to remember the kind of September

When life was slow and oh so mellow

Try to remember the kind of September

When grass was green and grain was yellow

Try to remember the kind of September

When I was a young and callow fellow

Try to remember

and if you remember

then follow

Jerry

Looking down into the mirror, I gazed into the neatly formed lines of the carefully strained rows of cocaine. The shiny plate glass was gingerly passed to me. I leaned down toward the "white magic," gently placing the three-inch-long straw slightly up my nose at one end, and at the other end, barely touching the "blow" or "snow" as it is referred to in the drug culture.

A quick sniff in each side of my already worn nostrils of this "avant-garde" — wonder high of today, will cure the blues — for a short time…a very short time. But on this occasion, I didn't glance up and start the inane "rap" with my recording artist friends around this very exclusive circle. Instead, I just continued to stare into the mirror and for the first time in a long time, I took a look at me. I hardly recognized myself.

I was married, but my wife hated me. I had a son, but he didn't know me.

What had I become? Where was the man I used to be?

Years ago, I had been a crusading Christian who dared to go against the tide in the music world. I took the message of hope to where I figured it was needed most — out where the people were. I knew that a man who fools around on his wife doesn't go into a Christian bookstore. He goes to a night club. So that's where my band and I went.

For 10 years we had an act like no other: fun, upbeat, with lots of audience interaction. And we always included, as a Seattle television producer once put it, "that Jesus stuff."

Then came our hit song, *Happy Days*. A year later, heady with success, I tried cocaine. Now I didn't even know myself.

Some of the great Christian men I had once worked with wouldn't recognize me either. Men like Bill Bright. When I met him in the '60s, I was a student at UCLA. His Campus Crusade for Christ evangelistic outreach ministry was already on 40 U.S. campuses and in two other countries. Under his direction, 100 men and women raised their own support so they could reach out to students full-time.* I got to know Bill personally while singing with the Kingsmen Four quartet that accompanied him to other college campuses.

He once shared the wisdom that helped make his ministry a success. "Once you feel God wants you to do something, go the extra mile and believe God will supply the means to make it happen."

Then there was Hal Lindsey, a former riverboat captain who knew the everyday hard-working side of

---

*Now there are 14,000 Campus Crusade for Christ staff, plus 101,000 trained volunteers in 163 countries.

life. I met him my sophomore year at UCLA when he came on staff for Campus Crusade. He made no bones about his faith. As surely as he used to knock a worker off the deck for disobeying orders, he now jumped at the chance to tell someone, "There's a lot to this clean way of living. There's inner peace and there's surety of heaven waiting for you on the other side."

"Wanna good time?" he'd ask a teen. "Try Jesus. You haven't had a good time until you know the Man who rocked my boat — who set me free — free from a going-nowhere life.

"Love the fast lane? Hey, I've been there — had the girls, drank hard. But nothing tops knowing you're loved by the One who loves all. You can go through your whole life and miss knowing that love. You miss all the great plans He has for your life, too. Toss your mooring line in with Jesus."

Hal was a true fisher of men.

Somehow, knowing Bill and Hal meant knowing I had a purpose. Part of that purpose, I believed, was to be like them.

And it was their words of encouragement that provided the wind in my sails the day my career in music began.

Actually, I had performed since I was a boy, singing on top of a turned-over box so I could reach the radio mike. My dad, a preacher, had a weekly radio show. With grandma, Mem, accompanying me on the piano, I would open wide and belt out the favorite hymns of the times. What a great way to start out, singing hymns.

Of course, my father wanted those hymns to mean more to me than just words and notes put together. When, at age 10, I gave my life into Jesus' authoritative hands, Dad smiled and stroked my head, "You make a difference for the Lord now, you hear?"

My grandparents also lived near us then, and they had a special impact on every day for my brother Kent and me. Pap, with his shock of black hair, and Mem, always in a print dress, celebrated life with singing, laughter and practical jokes. I guess they saw the same potential in me because they nicknamed me "Sunshine."

So, maybe I should say that gusts of inspiration from all these great men and women pushed me across the UCLA campus that fateful spring day of my junior year. I was headed back to the Spring Sing where our quartet, the Kingsmen Four, had performed earlier in the day. Suddenly, I bumped into Evan Williams so hard his glasses flew off.

"Jerry! You're the perfect guy!" he said.

"Perfect for what?" I laughed and handed him back his glasses.

"The Spring Sing…instrumental division. I paid the entry fee weeks ago but everyone's backed out on me. I need to put together a new group in a hurry. Will you help me?"

"How much time do we have?"

"Two hours."

I rubbed my hands together. This was terrific — my kind of challenge.

The Spring Sing was the annual competition of

musical talent collected from UCLA sororities and fraternities. Being located near Hollywood meant it was more than just another youth talent show. The judges were top composers and conductors, successful jazz musicians and actors, and top pop songwriters. This year even the president of Capitol Records was a judge. If you were shooting for the Hollywood stars, those judges could direct your aim dead center.

Evan took off for his fraternity and found a friend, Terry Smith, a 12-string guitarist, hanging around the living room. Terry knew of a banjo player and headed off to get him. The banjo player, Dave Fractman, brought along a friend he played with in a band, Kenny Ballard. And Chuck Stokes from my Kingsmen Four quartet was roped in as well. His deep bass voice would be yet another asset. All were born musicians. A spontaneous rehearsal was all they needed any time.

I made a bee-line for the Tri Delta sorority house. I knew a set of twins there who were well-known for their vocal blend. They'd be perfect. Not to mention, perfect to look at, too. I was especially drawn to the blonde, Susanne. I took her out on a date the year before, and she had been on my mind ever since.

You see, I dated a lot of girls. My sophomore year I made a personal challenge to see how many girls I could date in one year. By the end...120.

Often I went out with two in one day. One to a football game, another to the post-game party. I wanted to date as many girls as I could because I was determined to find out who was just right for me.

None compared with Susanne. Not only was she a beauty, but she had a quick wit, was charming in a crowd and, best of all, she, too, was a performer.

This would be my chance to perform with her on stage.

At first Susanne balked at the suddenness of it. But then, like a good sport, she said, "Why not. Diane and I would love to."

By the time we got the group together we totaled 10. Evan gave us the words to the chorus of "One, Two, Three" which we wrote on our forearms. We sang it through several times. Evan soloed on the verses backed by our *ooh's* and *ahh's*.

Just 15 minutes before going on, the master of ceremonies poked his head in. "What's the name of your group?" He had pen and paper in hand.

Everyone looked blank. I scanned our assortment. Although I was from Sigma Nu, most of the guys were from Sigma Alpha Epsilon fraternity. The campus joke was that they had few membership restrictions and, playing on their initials, we called the fraternity, "Somebody, Anybody, Everybody." Suddenly, inspiration hit. We were a musical hodgepodge and this was my chance to jab fraternity rivals.

I called out, "Somebody, Anybody, Everybody."

And that's how they introduced us that night to the celebrity judges seated front and center at the Hollywood Bowl. That's also the name they congratulated when we won not only our division but the overall sweepstakes. The judges said we were "the most outstanding musical act of the evening."

A Disneyland talent scout who was in the audience immediately booked us for a show. During the next year we played there many times, and our rehearsals at Terry Smith's house in Sherman Oaks brought us together like family. His parents, Helen and Dick, were Mom and Dad to all of us. In fact, Dick Smith instigated our first contract; singing a commercial for his employer, maker of the famous hair setting gel, Dippity-Do.

Our group narrowed from ten to seven committed members and they all proved ideal. Terry was not only an accomplished guitarist, but sang tenor as I did. Dave Fractman was the best banjo player around. Kenny looked like the classic California surfer, played guitar and delivered a smooth baritone. Chuck, with Art Garfunkel-like looks, was our dependable bass. Susanne and Diane sang precise harmonies and were instant eye catchers, smiling and dancing their way into everyone's hearts.

After Disneyland, we performed at fairs and hootenannies (coffee houses that featured folk music) up and down the California coast, plus two local TV shows.

As we toured, I watched the audiences react to our clean-cut style. Slowly, an idea began to form. We could give them more than a fun song — we could give them a message!

CHAPTER 2

Tonight, we're gonna fall in love

BY MIKE PRICE AND DAN WALSH

RECORDED BY PRATT & McCLAIN ON WARNER BROS. RECORDS

Tonight, tonight

   I hope it never ends

Tonight, we'll be

   Much more than just good friends

Tonight, tonight

   We're gonna fall in love tonight

Never before had I seen a guy dressed in such a mis-matched outfit: plaid pants, striped shirt, paisley tie, herringbone jacket and wing-tipped shoes. And to com-plete the look — a confident, cocky grin spread across his face.

I peeked from the second floor railing of my soror-ity house to see my blind date, Jerry McClain, then tip-toed back to my room.

"Let's play 'Name That Style' folks," I joked with my roommate, Bonnie. "Are we dressed to sweep a woman off her feet?"

In a low voice I answered myself, "Beep."

Bonnie giggled. "So, what are you going to wear, Susie?"

"I better wear one solid color so at least one of us looks like a normal person."

Although this McClain character had a reputation around campus as a hustler, our mutual friend who arranged this date thought otherwise. "You just couldn't meet a nicer guy," gushed Claudia when she first told me about Jerry. "You two would be perfect together. He's a good singer and fun at parties…and witty. Oh, you two are so much alike."

Now, as I pinned back my hair, I wished I could tell her, "Only one thing: his mother forgot to teach him how to dress."

Still, I was a little curious. How would this confident "alley cat" react to me? Most guys I dated were somewhat intimidated when they discovered that my twin sister and I had been singing for audiences since we were little. Of course, at first the audiences were as small as we were…small in number, that is.

It started when Diane and I skipped down the street in front of our house in Van Nuys, California. Whenever we saw Mr. Weaver cutting his hedges or Mrs. Weaver planting flowers, we'd stop and ask, "Do you have any song requests?" They knew how to play along and would good-naturedly listen to our enthusiastic attempts to imitate popular radio singers.

Then came singing and dancing lessons. Diane and I lived for those special Saturday mornings. We took the bus across town to Georgia Massey's storefront studio, pushed the door open and raced to be the first to get a hug from Georgia. Her hugs were warm and engulfing — especially engulfing since we were so little and her bosom was so large. I loved her right down to my toes! If she asked me to try harder during our lessons, I really gave it my all.

After lunch at home, we walked down to Stella Rae's studio where we were introduced to the world of theatre. Sometimes I barely took time for a sandwich because I wanted to get there to set up the stage or start the dress rehearsal for our next production. Neighbors came to our shows and applauded, and we truly felt like Broadway stars.

The lessons were a great expense to our hardworking parents, and we must have annoyed our brother Dennis endlessly with all our practicing at home. But it was worth it. By the time we entered high school in Claremont, California, Diane and I were writing songs and singing for teen dances. At the Battle of the Bands in our junior year, we even won "Best New Duo."

It pays to go public. A record company producer, Nick Venet (later the producer for Diana Ross) saw us at the Battle of the Bands and signed us to a contract on Keen Records. We couldn't believe it. He even let us record our own songs. I still have the 45s we made.

Yet the real feather in our cap came two years later. Our friend, Carolyn Bushnell, secretly entered both of us in the Los Angeles County Fair Queen Contest. It is the largest fair in the United States, so we didn't think we had a chance. Still, it sure was fun: taffeta dresses, ladies fixing our hair, meeting all the other girls.

The pivotal moment was when we were each privately interviewed by the judges. Diane looked tense when she went in. I, on the other hand, felt completely at ease.

Finally, Diane came out and the judges called me.

"Miss Roshay, we want you to answer two questions: why would you like to be queen of our fine Los Angeles County Fair, and what are your plans for the future?"

I pointed to the door where Diane and I had just passed each other. "Well, I'm her twin sister, so whatever Diane said...ditto."

They roared with laughter, and we won the crown. Two crowns, I mean — we were named co-queens. That meant we were the "glamour girls" photographed with the world's largest zucchini (no kidding). We also stood beside racing horses, milked cows, and, of course, waved from a Cinderella-like carriage during the daily parade.

It was a heady start and some guys didn't know what to make of my "success." I wondered how this Jerry McClain would handle it.

I skipped down the stairs in blue — all blue.

"I've planned a fabulous evening for us," he said. "Ready to go?"

Our first stop was a high school gym. We weren't there just to watch a game, though. Jerry was the coach. He really did a fine job, but I didn't tell him that.

Then, on to a church where, again, we weren't just part of the audience. When the speaker looked his way, Jerry jumped up — he was the entertainment. Soon he had the group laughing at his jokes, and then led them in a well-known chorus.

Before going on, he apologized, "You'll have to excuse me folks. My piano player wasn't able to make it tonight."

(I didn't know whether to believe him or not.)

"Say, Mom, could you come up and help me out?"

I swung my head around and saw a shy blonde woman (who did in fact look like Jerry) walking toward the front. His mother? On the first date I'm going to meet his mother? What more is he going to do to try and impress me?

Jerry then introduced the speaker and sat down beside me. After a few minutes he leaned over and whispered, "Because you're new here, they might call on you to give your testimony."

"Testimony?" I whispered back. "What's that?"

"You know, how you came to know the Lord. It only needs to be five or six minutes long." He drew out the "long."

I inwardly panicked. I didn't have a "testimony." I was Catholic. I'd known about God since catechism, but that wasn't anything to get up and tell a group of Protestants about.

To my relief, the meeting ended without any fingers pointing my way.

"I had you worried," Jerry laughed, driving away.

The last stop of our whirlwind date was his fraternity, Sigma Nu, for a party. Of course, Jerry was in charge — he was the social chairman (though he didn't drink). I also found out it was one of two hats he wore here. He was also the chaplain. Yes, this guy was going to take some figuring out.

Apparently Jerry wasn't too sure about me either, because we didn't see each other again until the following spring when he suddenly rushed into our sorority house and invited Diane and me to compete in the Spring Sing.

"Now? When it's already started?" I asked.

"Sure. With all the talent and harmony you two have, we're a sure win," he said.

The flattery worked, but, in the end, I knew it was the combined talent of our group of ten seasoned musicians that pulled off the victory.

The immediate requests to perform we received up and down the coast paved the way for Jerry and me to spend more time together. At each rehearsal and concert, my interest in Jerry grew. He was a thoughtful leader-type, always spiking a suggestion with a joke. We weren't actually a couple, though, until a baseball game sealed our fate.

"Oh, I'd never take a girl to a baseball game...she'd talk all the time."

"Well, I wouldn't," I volunteered. "I love watching baseball. I used to go all the time with my dad."

I proceeded to convince him that I knew the game well, so Jerry decided to take a gamble. The next Saturday we sat in Dodger Stadium. It was a hot July night. We talked baseball at first; Jerry was impressed. Then the conversation trailed off into his personal life...and mine. By the ninth inning our hot dogs lay on our laps, half-eaten, and we had no idea who won the game. But we both knew our hearts had scored home runs.

From then on we had a wonderful time together as our budding careers introduced us to entertainers we had previously only admired from afar — Everly Brothers, Jimmy Durante and Frankie Laine. Some were newcomers, like ourselves. Several times when we rehearsed in our manager's basement, John Deutschendorf would stop by. He and our guitarist, Kenny Ballard, had gone to Texas Tech together.

John would try out new songs he'd written. Once he couldn't decide on a name for one song in particular and asked our advice.

"Should I call it 'All My Bags Are Packed,' or 'Leaving on a Jet Plane'?"

We all voted for the latter. It was the first of many hits for John — John Denver, as he's known today.

After a year and a half of singing, traveling and falling in love, I thought marriage to Jerry was the next step.

However, Jerry had one reservation.

"I need to tell you something that's hard for me to say because I'm in love with you." He looked pale. "You see, I want God's plan for my life…exclusively. And since you haven't made Jesus your personal Savior, I can't marry you."

I held back the tears. "Jerry, I don't understand."

"Susanne, you know *of* the Lord, but you don't *know* the Lord. It's not a religion, it's a relationship that's missing."

He took me to a Campus Crusade meeting to show me what he meant. Hal Lindsey spoke. Holding a picture, he pointed to it and said, "Jesus is standing at the door of your heart, knocking — just like he's knocking symbolically on this wooden door. If you open the door of your heart, Jesus will come in."

I was confused. I was a Catholic, baptized and confirmed. Why did I have to do more? Wasn't I close enough to God?

Hal arranged for me to meet with his wife, Jan. She explained how many of the rules in the Catholic church weren't in the Bible, but were man-made. For example, I could confess my sins directly to God, anytime. I didn't need to go through a priest in a confessional booth.

As we sat together on her flowered couch, the faint fragrance of peanut butter trailed in from the kitchen. Her twin daughters were having a snack after school. Jan opened up a little white booklet titled, *My Heart, Christ's Home*. She began to read, "Jesus Christ will actually enter a heart, settle down, and be at home there."

Be at home...in my heart, I thought. My mind floated back to my childhood.

Even with a twin, a constant friend, I knew a loneliness I couldn't explain. One afternoon when I was a little girl, I was backstage after a play when a fear as real as a villain swept over me. I stood there, frozen, feeling utterly abandoned. It was as if I had no parents, no twin, no friends. Just me, alone.

That night I didn't want to go to sleep, afraid the fear would come again. I kept Diane giggling with jokes and antics until late. She finally said, "I can't keep my eyes open anymore. Good night. It's been fun."

I wanted to beg, "Please don't go to sleep. It might come on me again." My eyes darted around the dark room as I hugged my pillow.

Then it came again — like a devilish prowler — reminding me that in this world, I faced spiritual powers alone.

Jan Lindsey touched my arm. She was talking about how our heart is like a house with many rooms. "...and Jesus can fill every one, if you invite Him in."

She described our minds as the "library" — we choose to either put in good thoughts and influences or bad ones. The "dining room" was centered around selfishness unless we chose Jesus' diet of clean living.

When she read of the "drawing room," I warmed. It was here in the "withdrawing room" of my heart, Jan told me, that I could talk and be with Jesus daily. He would reveal the truth of the Bible to me. Here I would be reminded of His love.

Never alone again...if I chose to invite Jesus in.

"But you have a choice, Susanne," Jan said. Her perfume wafted through the air. "Jesus can either be a guest in your heart — or the master. If He's your Lord, you must give Him control of every area of your life. You seek what He wants, then do His bidding.

"It's a simple decision — but you must count the cost. We're all selfish. We'll always have to fight selfishness.

"But if Jesus is your Lord, you are assured you're going to heaven and your life here on earth is in His hands. You can rest in His care."

"I want to do that," I whispered.

Jan quietly looked at me, then gently took my hands in hers. "Let's pray," she said.

Right there, in the warmth of her living room, I prayed and, at my invitation, Jesus' spirit came upon me. The secret fear that had haunted me all those years dispelled instantly.

I finally met my dearest Friend.

I hurriedly called Jerry when I got back to my room. "I have Someone in my heart now," I cried. He was thrilled for me. (The whoop he let out was sure confirmation.)

The following August, with Jerry's persistent encouragement, I attended a Campus Crusade conference in Arrowhead Springs, California. They called it a Leadership Training Institute.

"You need to grow now that you're a Christian," Jerry told me. "And this is the place that turns seeds into sunflowers."

I didn't exactly blossom that first day. My first Bible study I felt sorely out of place. Seated in a circle, we were to each take a turn and pray aloud. I panicked. The only prayers I knew didn't sound appropriate. I tried them out under my breath: "Bless me Father for I have sinned…" No. "Hail Mary, full of grace…" No. "Bless us our Lord and these thy gifts…" Oh dear.

I felt even more awkward when they sent us out on the beach to practice witnessing. I had been brought up with the strict instruction that it wasn't proper to talk about religion, politics, or your age. Now they wanted me to burst into conversation with The Four Spiritual Laws!

I looked around and finally spotted someone sitting alone. By the water, facing the gentle lapping waves was a girl. How ferocious could she be?

I went over, sat down and faced her.

"Do you want to make Jesus your personal Savior?" I asked. "No, wait," I corrected myself. "That's number four. Let me back up," I smiled sheepishly. "Number one is 'God loves you and created you to know Him personally.' That's right."

She looked at me puzzled. "You want…what?"

"Oh, I don't want anything," I countered. "Well, I want…just…I mean I hope you might consider making…Jesus your Lord…like I have," I managed.

"Listen," she shook her head, "I'm Catholic and I don't think…."

"Oh good," I interjected. "Whew. I'm a Catholic too. I mean, I *was* a Catholic. Well, I still am, kinda. It's just that I went to a meeting with my boyfriend and…" I let out my breath. "Say…can I start over from the beginning?"

That was my first experience at witnessing. Afterward, I was exhilarated. Not because I did it all right, obviously. But because I was able to share this wonderful, new love I felt inside — a love that stayed with me every day, everywhere I went, burning like a warm fire. I wanted to spread that warmth not out of duty — but from sheer joy.

My life had begun — with Jerry — and with God.

CHAPTER 3

There's no business like show business

BY GEORGE AND IRA GERSHWIN

PERFORMED BY THE LIVELY SET ON THE LAWRENCE WELK SHOW

There's no business like show business

Like no business I know

Everything about it is appealing

Everything the traffic will allow

Nowhere can you get that happy feeling

When you are stealing that extra bow

You can learn a lot just watching the pros. And in 1966 I not only watched, I took notes...from pros like Don Rickles, Wayne Newton and Jerry Lee Lewis.

Now, I'm not talking about watching them on TV. I studied them in person, because suddenly we were performing at the same ritzy hotels and casinos in Lake Tahoe, Las Vegas, and Miami Beach. That's a big leap from the county fairs and hootenannies. And it was a member of the Beach Boys who gave us a running start. I met him one ordinary Monday when I simply went for a haircut.

I was telling my barber how, after our big win at UCLA's Spring Sing, our group had played steadily all over. We had just finished an engagement at Disneyland. The barber was impressed and glad for us. Better yet, so was the guy sitting next to me. He introduced himself as Bruce Johnston, a staff producer for Columbia Records. (He later became a member of the

Beach Boys.) In fact, he liked my description of our group so well he asked if we could drop by the studio the next day and record a demo tape. He said he would try to sell us to the "top dogs" (company executives).

Of course, I immediately said, "We'll be there." I hurriedly left the shop, jumped into my two-toned Chevy convertible, and raced to the house of our manager, Coffee Walker, in the wooded subdivision of Laurel Canyon. The other group members were just trickling in for rehearsal as I exploded with the good news.

The next morning was an eye-opening experience for me. In the recording studio I was surprised at how good I sounded. And it wasn't just my opinion. I was consistently picked for solos on the five songs we put down on tracks.

I personally considered this a sign — a confirmation. I once had dreamed of playing professional baseball like my hero Mickey Mantle, until I tore shoulder tendons while pitching for UCLA. With that door closed, I turned to my other passion: performing. I wasn't sure exactly how God wanted to use me in the entertainment business, but listening to the studio playback told me that at least I wasn't out of my league.

We finished the session and Bruce hand-delivered the demo tape to his bosses. In a few days, the verdict was back — we sounded too much like their New Christy Minstrels.

Undaunted, Bruce called a friend at Mercury Records. Their response was more to our liking — they wanted us. We were on our way.

At UCLA's Spring Sing that year we made quite a sensation when we returned as successful alumni. We introduced our newly recorded "Try to Remember" and debuted a Roaring '20s medley of three bouncy, banjo tunes: "Bill Bailey," "Hold That Tiger," and "Just Because."

Like the year before, powerful Hollywood personalities were everywhere. Immediately after the concert some of that power pushed our way. Billy McDonald, an agent with Associated Booking (who'd just signed an unknown singer named Barbra Streisand) shook our hands backstage and assured us it was just a matter of working out the details 'til our names were up on marquees.

First came TV cameras. Billy set us up to work on ABC's dance show, "Shivaree," co-hosted by Sonny and Cher. The husband and wife team was presently riding high with their #1 hit "I Got You Babe."

When we showed up at the studio, Susanne joked, "I'm not getting into one of those." Suspended cages for go-go dancers hung on the set. We were to sing from a spotlighted platform, to Susie's relief, surrounded by dancing teenagers.

Standing next to Sonny and Cher, we looked unusually tidy. The two wore wild outfits: bobcat fur jackets, slacks with multicolored striped patterns, beaded necklaces and long hair.

Backstage, I talked with Sonny and learned the reasoning behind their way-out look: it made them unique. They weren't a band like the vastly popular Beatles, nor into the drug culture like the Grateful

Dead. They were a duo — only one of many at that time. To be noticed they had to be different. So he and his wife took the fashions of the day a step beyond anyone else and designed their own outlandish clothes. People noticed!

So I took note: clothes make a statement.

After "Shivaree," we actually did get our name on a marquee…as headliners no less! We changed our name to The Lively Set (Somebody, Anybody, Everybody wouldn't fit — too many letters). When the janitor at the Riviera Hotel in Las Vegas arranged the marquee for our next engagement, he must have gotten his instructions mixed up because he put our names in big letters and the stars of the show, Dan Rowan and Dick Martin of "Laugh-In" fame, in small letters. We loved it. Susanne ran out and snapped a picture before the real stars discovered the mistake and made the hotel change it.

Las Vegas was a huge classroom for me. Every casino, every hotel had a name to send the eyebrows up. It was like a huddle of modern-day vaudeville theatres.

At the plush International Hotel I was forever changed after seeing legendary Jerry Lee Lewis. Influenced early by blues and boogie players in his native Ferriday, Louisiana, he played like such a dynamo you thought the piano keys would explode. And that was with one hand. With the other, he took off his jacket and tie and shoved away the piano bench, sending it skidding across the stage, all the while belting out "Great Balls of Fire" and his body moving in every conceivable position.

I watched him sing his hits from the '50s: "Whole Lotta Shakin' Goin' On," "Breathless," "High School Confidential," plus many of his new country songs like "What Made Milwaukee Famous (Has Made a Loser Out of Me)." And I made another note: crowds liked action, the wilder the better.

Then there was Wayne Newton — a showman extraordinaire. His trademark was variety. He switched from piano to guitar to violin to trumpet with music ranging from rock to country to classical to romantic.

Wayne and his older brother, Jerry, performed six shows a night, six nights a week at the Fremont Hotel. They were in better physical shape than some athletes. The first half of his show was constant and intense. Yet, here again, Wayne demonstrated a master's use of variety as he then slowed down the pace, talking to the audience, crooning to a pretty girl.

He wasn't really a master instrumentalist — it just looked that way. His chord changes were all basic. But by knowing the basics of a lot of instruments he looked like an amazingly versatile talent. I left his show determined to learn the fundamentals of a few more instruments so I could add variety to our act.

Back in our dressing room at the Riviera, we got a call from Billy, our agent. He said Dean Martin and his producer, Greg Garrison, caught our opening before Rowan & Martin and wanted us for his popular variety show. We'd tape in February.

Most people think Dean Martin acted the part of a drunk. We found out otherwise. After we performed our number, Dean came on and stood between the twins. Well, tried to stand. He was staggering. Susanne told me later it was all she could do to sing, smile and hold up Dean. Plus he was totally unrehearsed. The girls had to feed him the lines to the song we had ironically chosen, "Come On, Get Happy."

The next day we flew to Chicago and performed a show for 10,000 conventioneers. Then it was on to Lake Tahoe. There we met "Mr. Warmth" himself, Don Rickles. We'd been signed to a multi-year contract to open for Rickles because we provided a needed contrast. Some considered his act coarse, even vulgar. We were to add a family touch, helping attract a broader range of customers.

Many saw Rickles only as a short, stocky, balding Jewish comedian with a nasty mouth. However, offstage he was a sweet, considerate, happily married man. "Mr. Warmth" really was his true character.

He could read people like a master psychologist. He'd make fun of their size, their shape, their color, blatantly hitting them below the belt. Yet the "victims" laughed. He took skeletons right out of the closet — things that divide people: prejudices, greed, ignorance — and audiences realized how ridiculous those skeletons looked. By stabbing at what was bad, he overtly pointed to what was good.

After our twenty-minute show, the audience applauded enthusiastically. Don clapped, too, and said,

"Isn't the Lively Set great?" Then he turned to his con-
ductor, Bobbie Crow, and said flatly, "Would you get
them some cookies and milk?"

He turned back to us, "This is no Disneyland, you
know. We serve drinks here."

For performances, we wore green polka dot shirts
with white pants. "Let's hear it for the Lively Set," he'd
say, then wave us away. "Ah, ya' look like a bunch of ice
cream salesmen."

News-making sports figures and movie stars loved
it when he picked on them. Don would make them get
up on stage, do a spontaneous, embarrassing skit, then
ask, "Are you breathing on me? Because, if not, my
socks are rolling down."

Sitting at a front table in the audience was always
dangerous. One night he picked on a southerner.

"Where you from?" he asked the eager tourist.

"Louisville, Kentucky."

"What's your name?"

"Carnavelas.

"Carnavelas? I had that in the Navy. It starts out as
a rash."

Don pointed to the woman at the table. "Is this
the wife?" The man nodded "yes" and Don turned to the
orchestra and flipped his hand in a "so-so" sign. Then
he walked back toward her, looking meek, took her
hand and kissed it. He suddenly pulled away with a gri-
mace.

"What'd you have for dinner? Fish?"

At the end of his show, the "insult master" revealed

his soft heart. "All I can tell you is enjoy life and never forget your mother, be she in eternity or here on this earth. She'll never forget you, I swear to that. Good night, Mom in Florida, and may God give you strength."

Our life on the road was great. We played all day, performed at night, and slept in plush hotel rooms. As kids in our early 20s we thought it couldn't get any better. But it did.

Bob Banner, producer of "The Carol Burnett Show," was looking for young undiscovered talent to be on a NBC summer musical variety show called "The Kraft Music Hall."

The show originated on radio in 1933 with hosts like Bing Crosby. Then it crossed over to television. The music-hall format was introduced with Milton Berle starring in "The Kraft Music Hall" in 1958, providing an hour of entertainment: singers, comedians, actors.

During the summer of 1966, Banner wanted to emphasize young talent, so he chose handsome, dimpled singer John Davidson as host. He also thought we might be right for the show and asked us to audition.

I was uneasy about the audition. Perhaps if we'd had more notice, I would have relaxed. But we were on our way to a month-long engagement at a Florida hotel and only had time to squeeze in the Kraft agent's office. Because we were in a rush, I thought we came off unpolished. I was sure we made our worst impression.

I was dead wrong. They put our names on the 13-week contract as soon as we walked in the door. Our friendliness, clean-cut look and the novelty of the twins — our image alone sold them. When they saw we were also impromptu performers the deal was secure.

During the first rehearsal they asked, "Who arranged that bit you did at the audition?" The group turned and pointed to me.

"Okay. We want you on the show's writing staff. (I guess it pays to watch the pros!) He also asked Terry to be in the think tank and directed us to a room where we were joined by (then newcomers) George Carlin and Richard Pryor.

The show was musical variety. John sparkled the camera with his all-American smile and introduced the cast: comedians George Carlin and Richard Pryor, singers Jackie and Gayle (from The Christy Minstrels), The Five King Cousins (daughters of The King Sisters), The Jimmie Haskell Orchestra, our group and a special guest for the week, people like Flip Wilson, the Ace Trucking Company, Jimmy Rodgers, Everly Brothers, Gary Lewis and The Playboys.

A favorite every week was a visit from the "Hippie Dippie Mailman" (George Carlin). He'd read a letter out loud, slowly, like his brain was permanently drugged.

"You've got a letter here…from Iowa…John. He wonders why…your hair never moves."

George was also the "Hippie Dippie Weatherman."

"There's going to be clouds…and lots of rain….
So if you're going out, you'll see…clouds and…rain."

I especially liked the spontaneity of the last segment of the show — at least it appeared spontaneous. The audience was seated around cocktail tables to resemble a nightclub. John walked out among the guests and asked couples "What year did you fall in love?" They'd say, "1958," for example.

"Then you'll remember songs like..." and John sang several popular songs from that year in a medley. The couples were always amazed that he picked their favorites and wondered how Jimmie Haskell's orchestra could play along so spontaneously. Actually, John and the orchestra had prearranged the songs they would use for each year so their only trick was pulling out the right bundle of sheet music.

I filed the idea away for future reference.

Richard Pryor, a brash kid from Gary, Indiana, was unlike anyone on the cast. We found out what set him apart when the fire department was called in.

Susanne and Diane were in their dressing room when they smelled an odd odor. It reminded them of singed hair in a blow dryer. They called security and said they suspected an electrical fire somewhere in the building. Without delay, security called the fire department.

The firefighters traced the smell to the dressing room next to the girls' and bolted in the door. Richard Pryor stood amidst a cloud of smoke, leaning against the bathroom door frame. The toilet was flushing behind him.

"Hey, man, what's happenin'?" he asked, sluggishly.

The firemen ushered the girls out. "I don't think you have anything to worry about. Everything will be all right."

Richard's drug use showed up in the conference room, too. Terry had written a commercial and he, George Carlin, Richard and I were working out a comedy sketch to lead into it. Richard pulled out a joint and asked if we'd like to join him.

We brushed him off and got back to work. Afterward I talked privately with Bob Banner about the incident. Richard never made his habit public again.

I later found out Terry would have gladly accepted Richard's offer. Our group portrayed a clean-cut image, but it was another story for him and one of our other guitarists, Dave Fractman, in their motel rooms.

After we completed "Kraft Music Hall," we appeared dock-side at Pier 66 in Fort Lauderdale, Florida. Our first night there Terry and Dave took new girlfriends to their rooms and the smell of marijuana drifted through the halls.

It was a difficult predicament. I was only one of seven with a voting voice. Even though we were all friends, they told me I didn't have a right to impose my convictions on them.

The next night Mrs. John D. Rockefeller III saw our show and invited us out on their yacht. She asked about my positive approach to life and, with newly fueled zeal, I pulled out a *Four Spiritual Laws* booklet from my wallet and told her of my faith. She was delighted, telling me she was a Christian herself. We met her teenage children and, wanting to make the most of the opportunity, I invited them to come with us to hear Hal Lindsey speak on end-time prophecy the next night at a University of Miami Campus Life meeting directed by Eddie Waxer. The Lively Set was to open the meeting with songs.

The Rockefellers liked Hal and vice versa. I wasn't surprised — most people liked him, including Terry and Dave. Those two just didn't want to change their ways. They were preparing for the coming judgment Hal talked about — but going in the wrong direction.

That night I woke up in a cold sweat. I paced the dark room not able to shake a nightmare. I dreamt my life didn't count for Christ.

Every day I prayed for God's guidance and, more recently, for each member of our group. Now, because of the dream, I felt at a crossroads. Would I have to make some major changes in order to follow God's call for my life?

Our act was an obvious musical success. At the same time, Hal's meetings made me realize the importance of sharing my faith. Could the two be combined? Could we do a night club act plus tell people about salvation? It wasn't being done in Las Vegas, that's for sure.

Part of the answer came when we returned to California. Bill Bright, Campus Crusade's founder, called and asked me to come to Arrowhead Springs and help to train their traveling musical ministry, The New Folk (also known as Armageddon Experience). The group was in rehearsal and he thought I could spice up the arrangements.

I walked in ready to take charge: fresh from NBC studios, TV veteran, bold spiritual witness to the Rockefellers. It was obvious — I was the man they needed.

Seems like I was the only one who recognized "the obvious," because no one in the room noticed me. They were corraled around a dark, curly-headed guy at the piano. Miffed, I pushed down a velvet-cushioned theater seat and waited until someone came up for air.

"Girls," the piano man instructed, "you come in on the eighth bar and back Bob up with a chorus of *ahh's.* Then your part goes…" (He sang a passable soprano.)

"While they're doing that, you baritones will go like this…" (Not bad pitch on that either.)

"The intro on the piano sounds like this…" (he played a run of notes), "…so you guitars start in G. The second time through we'll go up a half a step." (Who was this guy?)

I couldn't wait any longer. I cleared my throat loudly.

Bob Horner finally noticed me. "Jerry! Glad you could make it. Come meet The New Group."

I was introduced to the curly-headed mastermind — Michael Omartian.

And they did need my help with the format of the show. I suggested they create suspense by starting with the drums for four measures, then add the guitars, then a tambourine….

Out of the corner of my eye I saw Michael scribbling furiously. Still talking, I nonchalantly walked his way and peered over his shoulder. He was writing everything down — all the parts. Man, with that kind of initiative we could have the first bit worked out by noon. I suggested a break to let Michael finish. Besides, Bob and I had some catching up to do. However, we hadn't gotten past the weather when Michael passed out new scores.

"Ah, was your name Jerry?"

I nodded.

"Guess we're ready."

What would have taken me hours, took Michael mere minutes.

By afternoon I knew Michael's history. He was a musical prodigy — at 9, he wrote a symphony; by 12, he was writing arrangements for the high school band. Although his family wanted him to be a doctor, his kinship with the Lord told him to invest the musical talents he'd been given.

If I had a guy like that in my band...an idea started to take shape. His talent coupled with devotion to God....

When I got back home to L.A., I was forced to be more practical. Our group hit a cold spot. Suddenly, a clean-cut act wasn't so hot and we could only get weekend dates. I didn't have much to offer Michael careerwise, but we talked by phone weekly and I told him I'd look for an opportunity to get him started.

As The Lively Set, however, the clock was about to

strike midnight. I thought of one man who might keep us going — clean-cut was always "in" with him. Every week on national TV, Lawrence Welk proudly displayed his philosophy: "I stick with what I do and don't change with the times."

Actually, I had met Mr. Welk years before. Right after my baseball injury I walked onto his lot at ABC Studios. During a break in taping, I introduced myself.

"Hello. I'm Jerry McClain. I'm a student at UCLA and I think I'd be perfect for your show."

He graciously asked me to audition on the spot and I sang "Scarlet Ribbons."

"You've got talent," he assured me. "You just need more experience. Come back and see me."

So, I was ready to try again, this time with a record and a portfolio of big-name associations. Even our county fair days came in handy. We had worked with several from his cast: the dance team, Bobbie and Cissy, Guy and Ralna, and the Lennon Sisters. I called them first and they encouraged me to pitch our group to Mr. Welk. Nervous, but wearing my best confident smile, I walked into the Hollywood Palladium, where he was warming up his band for their regular Saturday night dance.

The gaudy dance hall was a flashback to another generation. One, I hoped, with room for us. Mr. Welk was glad I'd gotten experience and he took into account the recommendations from his cast. In a matter of minutes he agreed to hire us for two shows.

We rehearsed Monday through Thursday and taped

on Friday. It impressed me that Lawrence Welk surrounded himself with talented people and was always eager to put them in the spotlight. That was his charm. Not the center of attention, he was more a director of attention.

I can't say we agreed with all of Mr. Welk's opinions, though. For example, he didn't approve of the girls' dresses. For our Roaring '20s routine, the girls had Ret Turner, designer for Cher and Carol Burnett, make them flapper dresses. Over a sheer orange slip hung black sparkling strips that flew around like streamers on a Maypole when they danced the Charleston. Mr. Welk only noticed that the dresses ended two inches above their knees.

"Their dresses can't be any shorter than what the Lennon Sisters wear," Mr. Welk insisted.

Susanne and Diane pleaded with him for half an hour, showing him that there wasn't a hem to let out and mentioning the price tag: $2,000. The girls won him over.

All in all, we loved working for Mr. Welk and hoped for a long run. But he kept a tight budget and decided he could afford only four of us on a permanent basis.

How could we choose who got the boot? It seemed unethical. We started together, we'd end together. We decided it was time for our chariot to turn back into a pumpkin. Most of The Lively Set went on to other jobs or to finish school.

During that summer I had time to process all I had experienced during the past year. I felt like I was collecting parts of a script about to be filmed. Then one unforgettable evening, Hal Lindsey helped the picture develop.

We drove to San Francisco and, after he spoke at a fraternity, we walked in and out of the nightclubs surrounding the Berkeley campus. Hal wanted to be brought up to date. For me each band solidified my conviction.

At Bill Graham's Fillmore West we saw Jefferson Airplane, The Grateful Dead and Janis Joplin. They blared out pounding, disjointed notes and unintelligible lyrics. Day-Glo-painted freaks milled around vats of Kool-Aid mixed with LSD.

We then walked toward Haight-Ashbury Park, a hippie haven. Marijuana joints were being shared everywhere, men kissed each other without shame, groups of young teens huddled around bottles of cheap wine. A bearded hippie wearing a white robe passed us. Behind him trailed flower-throwing girls — his "disciples." We watched as he led them up the hill, stood still a moment, triumphantly, then dropped his robe. Hal gasped. A swaying young "disciple" with long, blonde hair opened her arms to him. He pulled her close, pressing their bodies together.

We turned away, sickened.

"It's like Sodom and Gomorra." Hal looked down at his shoes.

I motioned to a park bench and we sat down. "You know, Hal, we have every right to be as bold as they are!"

"What do you mean?" Hal asked, confused and a little surprised.

I hurried to make myself clear. "Hal, I want to do popular music but give the message of Christ at the same time."

Hal sat back on the bench. I continued. "Think about it. Tonight The Grateful Dead openly told kids to smoke pot...like it was the answer to every human need. The Beatles — they say Mahareshi has given them true peace. Nobody questions it. Cat Stevens is out saying Hinduism is where it's at. Because they entertain, they can say anything. I want to turn that around for the good."

"What do you have in mind?"

I had wanted to tell Hal about my idea for a long time. The air felt still. I rose and rubbed my hands together under the brightness of the streetlight.

"I see it in my mind...like I'm watching a movie," I told Hal.

"We'll do shows in night clubs. We'll be so good, so fun, so cool, the audience will be right there." I held out my open palm. Then cupping it like a camera lens I put it in front of my eye.

"I see a middle-aged man, sitting at a little round cocktail table. The stage lights glisten off his yellowed teeth. He claps along with our music."

I moved my "camera" to Hal's left. "An airline stewardess sits at another table. She's worn out and disillusioned with life in the fast lane. But she stares at us, captivated, not daring to blink, afraid she'll miss something."

I zoomed to Hal's other side. "Beside her is her boyfriend, a good-looking pilot. He's not looking at us any more because he's lost in his own thoughts. Tears are in his eyes. He pictures his wife and kids back home, realizing how much he misses them, how good family life really is, and how crummy he is for cheating on them so many years. He sees for the first time how his unchecked ego has led him from one shallow affair to another."

I dropped my lens and looked at Hal squarely. "Hal, Jesus shed his blood for these people — for lonely hearts everywhere." Tears mingled with the sweat dripping down my face. "We've got to reach them. It's unfair not to tell them. But we have to go to them, get their attention even while they have a drink in one hand and a half sober mind. A heart can never be drunk, only broken."

I paced. "Jesus said if we're only friendly to our friends we're no different than heathens. We, as Christians, have to reach people outside the church walls — and this is the way I think God wants me to do it, through my music."

I sat down. "I don't know how to make it happen yet, but that's my dream."

We sat quietly under the light. After several minutes passed, I suddenly felt self-conscious about my outburst. I looked over at Hal, "Sounds crazy, huh?"

He didn't say anything at first. Then his warm hand firmly gripped my shoulder. "God has given you this dream. You have to do this." His voice cracked with emotion. "God will help you make it happen."

Hal gave me the confirmation I needed. I could make my life count for Christ — and through the music I loved. The future suddenly seemed full of endless opportunities.

I decided to get a few things settled in my personal life. I went back to school — I felt I owed it to my family to finish college and get my degree. And, most important, I proposed to Susanne. I wasn't sure where I was headed, but I wasn't going anywhere without her.

CHAPTER 4

We'll walk with God

with God

WORDS ADAPTED BY JAN LINDSEY FROM THE STUDENT PRINCE

DUET WE SANG TO EACH OTHER AT OUR WEDDING

We'll walk with God, from this day on

> *His helping hand, we'll lean upon*

This is our prayer, our humble trust

> *May the Lord be ever with us*

Susanne

Just when you think everything's going for you it suddenly stops. At least it did after we got married.

Not the romance, mind you. Although all the catastrophies at our wedding made me wonder if romance was ever going to come.

It wasn't just that I was 40 minutes late to the church because I decided to follow the directions I included in our invitations.

It wasn't just that Hal Lindsey lost our marriage license right before he married us.

It wasn't just that Jerry's brother Kent couldn't drive us to the airport because he was burning up with fever.

It wasn't just that my brother Dennis offered to drive us, waved my folks off, with my luggage in their trunk and the keys to Dennis' car in my mother's purse.

And it wasn't just that people on the highway laughed and pointed at us as we drove with a "Just Married" sign. People were pointing and laughing at me, in particular, in the backseat. Perched on my lap was the ironing board and iron that had been used on my wedding dress and later stashed in the car we were crammed in. Guess they thought it was safe to heckle the "little housewife" a car's width away. Jerry didn't look much more suave. He was squeezed into the front seat with my sister (who held together the wires that were keeping the car running), and her boyfriend (who was driving madly to help us retrieve my luggage and catch the plane).

No, what made me wonder if romance would ever come was when we finally got to our Las Vegas hotel room. My sister had arranged to have her hand-made gift, a commemorative pillow, placed in our room. It was on the bed. One of the beds. There were two. Twin beds.

Jerry shook his head at the bell boy. "This will never do."

He'd waited a long time for this night. We went together four years before he proposed on Valentine's Day, 1968. I had been having such a good time living with my sister and two roomates that I hesitated.

"You're not ready yet?" Jerry was hurt.

"I need to think about it," I answered.

I thought about all Jerry brought into my life: the fun, the family. Out on the road with The Lively Set, I met many of his relatives. When we were in Texas his aunts (Nellie, Madie and Melba) wrapped their arms around me and told me story after story about how their prayers had brought miracles to their families. And I met the Dobsons — the Beaumont, Texas side of the family that raised popular Christian psychologist Dr. James Dobson.

In Florida, I met Jerry's father's side of the family.

At a small church in Bradenton, his preacher uncle stopped in the middle of the service and called, "Jerry Purl, get on up here and sing with me. I'm gonna play my saxophone and you bring all those kids up here with you."

His mother, Doris, was sweet and gentle. I liked her instantly — even though I didn't expect to meet her on our first date.

I felt especially close to his grandparents. Mem and Pap adopted me right away. At Sunday dinner, a month after we started dating, Pap announced, "I think I've come up with the perfect name for our little Susanne here. She's so full of sunshine like you, Jerry, we'll call her Sunette."

After lunch, Mem presented me with her favorite frying pan so I could make black-eyed peas and okra properly.

"Those Teflon pans won't do," she warned. It had to be a Texas, iron, scorch-it-till-it's-burned pan.

So, after two weeks of thinking about his proposal, I gave Jerry my answer.

"Well, I'm not sure who I love more — you or your grandparents. But we'll just say it's you."

A month later we used Easter traditions to help us make the wedding announcement to our families. I wrote it out in phrases and put the slips of paper in plastic Easter eggs. It was hilarious watching the grown-ups down on their hands and knees as they searched behind the television set, under the couch and out in the flower beds. The excited finders huddled together and read the message in numbered order.

"This is to…"

"…announce that…"

"…Jerry and Susanne…"

"…will be…"

"…getting married…"

"…August 10th."

After a weekend honeymoon (which really was romantic), we continued our summer engagement at Disneyland. What a dream world. We performed with so many big names (with big talents to match):The Four Freshman, Kenny Rogers, Pat Paulson, Patti Page, Vic Damone and Phyllis Diller. Every night, both on stage and in the night sky, we watched the fireworks.

Then it stopped. The phone stopped ringing off the hook. No more two-week engagements strung back to back. We played only weekend gigs.

Our popularity wasn't all that was coming apart. The country was in chaos. There were riots in the streets, demonstrations on campuses, both Dr. Martin Luther King, Jr. and Senator Robert Kennedy were assassinated, and the music reflected the changes. Our style of feel-good folk songs was out and the Bob Dylan-protest-type songs were in.

Jerry needed to finish school anyway and I had a teaching degree in music to fall back on. So I set out looking for work with fond memories of my student-teaching days at an upscale Santa Monica school. It would be great to be surrounded by little adoring children again.

However, because of such short notice, the only teaching position open was for 4th grade at a south-central L.A. public school in Watts. I took it.

The first morning of school a fight broke out on the playground.

First day jitters, I told myself.

The two boys were at each other's throats fighting over a ball. A crowd of kids gathered around, urging them on.

I pulled back the smaller of the two. "Stop this," I insisted. "You go get the ball and we'll go in and talk about this."

"Get it yourself, Whitey!" he spat. The surrounding faces sneered at me. Above their heads the windows were barred.

I felt ill-equipped to face their violent anger. I was equally baffled as to how I could make school better for them. I stood in front of my classroom of 32 squirming, bickering nine- and ten-year-olds with fewer supplies than they had.

And what they had, they often "lost." Stealing was rampant. Half my class couldn't eat lunch. They told me they "lost" it on the way to school.

Worst of all, they hated me.

Back at our apartment, Jerry was the opposite on the emotion pendulum swing. He was so excited about what he was learning in his political science classes, he kept me up nights talking about how he wanted to become an attorney.

It seemed unfair. When I came home all I wanted

to become was horizontal, on the couch.

Every day I drove home crying and praying, "Lord, get me outta here."

I know He heard my prayer, because I answered the phone call that turned us back into entertainers. Terry Smith, from our Lively Set group, said a Hollywood producer, Anita Kerr, was trying to find us. She remembered seeing our act two years before on "The Kraft Music Hall" and now wanted us for Standard Oil commercials she was producing.

I pulled down a string of garland from our Christmas tree and danced in celebration.

Anita and her husband, Alex Grob, came to our apartment and we signed the contracts. Starting in January, for four months, we were to write, sing and act in commercials. We'd also make personal appearances at clubs and fairs, doing our Lively Set act. And, as part of the company's promotional strategy we would focus patrons' attention on the beauty of America (and hope they got the hint to fill up on gas so they could see the sights). Our new name was "The American Scene."

A week later, John Denver called. Would we like to play Aspen and Vail during the holidays, a week at each resort town?

It was a glorious way to celebrate our re-entry into the music world.

Except John was melancholy.

He'd produced his own album, sure he'd never get a record company to sign him, and handed us each an autographed copy grimly.

"I'm on the way out," he said.

"Oh, you can't give up, John." I drew close. "I thought it was over for us, too. I was miserable and praying every day for God's help. Then Terry called with the news of this great deal with Anita Kerr. And you called, giving us two weeks at Christmas time in the Colorado mountains. Your call helped answer my prayer."

I don't know if John ever did become a praying man, but we knew the hand of God was leading us back into show business.

CHAPTER 5

The American scene

BY ANITA KERR

RECORDED BY THE AMERICAN SCENE ON DOT RECORDS

Let's make the scene

> *The American Scene*

It's a groovy scene

> *The American Scene*

C'mon let's go

> *You don't need dough*

To make the scene

> *The American Scene*

The Standard Oil commercials portrayed us as ideal youth — hip yet happy. (A contrast to the forlorn "flower children.") We danced around gas pumps — very clean, cherry red gas pumps — on a Hollywood set of pure white, like all-American cheerleaders. We even formed a pyramid.

We sang about all the wonderful sights to see in America. At Standard Oil gas stations across the country, customers were given postcards (the number depended on how much gas they bought). One side of the card pictured a beautiful American scene — Niagara Falls, Mt. Rushmore, Grand Canyon — and the other side showed us, with short white dresses and red lettered sweatshirts, "The American Scene." The postcard had a detachable stub the customer scratched with a coin to see if he won a new car or a trip to one of the pictured sights.

Besides writing, singing, and acting in the commercials, we made an industrial movie to remind those in the business what a fine company Standard Oil was. And, at conventions, we personally met and entertained gas station owners, corporate executives and stockholders. Although we had changed our name to The American Scene, we used our old Lively Set arrangements and the conventioneers loved it.

This promotional campaign was our ticket back to the big league entertainment spots — Las Vegas, Miami Beach, Lake Tahoe — we hit them all again. The more we promoted, the more bookings we got. The more bookings we got, the more Standard Oil was promoted.

In Las Vegas we were to appear in the main showroom of The Flamingo Hotel with Gene Barry, the star of the popular TV western "Batt Masterson."

Mr. Barry asked us to come to his house to practice. We went intending to rehearse a script prepared by his writers. However, Gene asked us to start off the rehearsal with our usual 20-minute show. He wanted to see what we were like. So we gave him our show right there in his blue living room with the tall wood-framed windows behind us. After we finished Mr. Barry turned and scowled at his writers. They buckled under his glare. They had written a show and Gene made it obvious he liked ours better.

Awkward as it was for them, the writers asked to use our material with Gene singing all the male leads. Some additional material was needed. Could we help with that too? We were happy to oblige.

Now I saw my chance to include Michael Omartian. He could make short work of new arrangements. My mind was spinning with ideas and Michael was just the man to make them come to life.

I called Michael as soon as we got back from Gene

Barry's house. This was the chance we'd both been waiting for. I'd get him into show business and he'd help me get a hit record. A hit record from a Las Vegas show? I was sure of it. As soon as Anita Kerr saw Michael's genius, she'd sign him on the dotted line as well.

But first, Michael had to go back to Campus Crusade's headquarters in Arrowhead Springs for an important meeting with Bill Bright. We made plans to meet in Nevada to prepare for our opening the next Tuesday.

Friday morning I headed down to the Musician's Union in Hollywood feeling like carefree Tom Sawyer, about to start a new adventure. All I needed to do was report the names of the musicians in The American Scene and pay the dues for the upcoming engagement — it was Union law. I quickly listed the names…then I thought of Michael. This was his first professional job — he wasn't a Union musician!

I rushed to the pay phone and called Arrowhead Springs. I convinced the operator that I had to talk to Michael. He finally came on the line.

"Michael, you have to get down here right away and join the Union. I'll pay your dues, just come and fill out these papers. If you leave immediately there will be just enough time before the office closes."

"I can't come now, Jerry. I'm in an important meeting with Bill Bright."

Didn't he get it? "Listen Michael, you can't come to Las Vegas and conduct the orchestra unless you join today." A lady walking by turned and stared at me. I was almost shouting by this time.

Michael was Mr. Calm. "Jerry, I know you'll take care of it somehow." And he hung up.

I didn't know what to do at first — until it was clear there was no other option.

I went home, put on a different shirt, grabbed a Chicago Cubs baseball hat and went back to the Union. I stepped up to a different window with a different clerk.

"Hello, I'm Michael Omartian and I need to join the Union." I gave her my best smile. "I'm a piano player. What papers do I need to fill out?"

She handed me a form. I quickly filled in his name and address...but his social security number?...his mother's maiden name? It had been five years since I applied. I forgot all the personal information they required. I told the girl I'd be right back; I had to go to the bathroom.

Around the corner and out of view, I dashed to the phone. This time I whispered, cupping the phone in my hands. "I'm Michael's insurance agent and it's very important that we get some information from him right away."

"He can't be disturbed."

"I know that — I mean, in that case, could you write these questions on a piece of paper, slip it to him in his meeting and then come back and tell me his written answers?"

"Why are you whispering?"

I jiggled the phone. "We must have a bad connection. You sound far away. Do I sound okay to you?"

"Yes, but you're whispering."

"Good. Would you please take him these questions?"

I guess she gave up trying to figure me out, because when she finally came back on the line she had all the information I needed.

I walked back down the hall and around to the clerk.

I put my hand on my stomach and said, "I had some problems."

She looked concerned.

I was pale, but not for the reason she was thinking of. Anyway, it worked to my advantage. "I hope you feel better," she said.

"I'll be okay, thank you. I have my money. Do I sign right here?"

"After your audition. What time should I put you down for?"

I went from pale to chalky white. Their policies had changed since I had signed up several years earlier as a bass player. I could bluff my way through almost anything, but play piano like Michael Omartian? What was I going to do?

"Three o'clock," I mumbled. It'd give me a few hours to think.

By three I had a plan, but there was a good chance it wouldn't work. I sized up the stern, old, has-been musicians who sat waiting to judge me. Oh well, I figured, if it falls through, I'll just confess the truth.

I sat down at the piano and saw sheet music which they obviously presumed I'd play.

I looked up at them with tired eyes and suggested a change. "Gentlemen, I've been in rehearsals all day with Anita Kerr. We're preparing for a big show. I'm beat. Would you mind if I just played something soothing, something...classical?"

Their pleasantly surprised expressions gave me the leeway I was counting on. They saw me now as someone who appreciated really good music.

I closed my eyes and started "Moonlight Sonata." On the fifth bar, I opened them and dramatically looked at each man, with feeling for the music. Then I squeezed my eyes shut and tossed my head down in a rush of emotion.

I was on the 30th bar when the oldest gentleman put his hand on my shoulder and said, "That's fine, Mr. Omartian." His voice was calm. "It's obvious you're an accomplished musician. We'd be proud to have you in our Union."

Thank goodness he stopped me on the 30th bar. I didn't know a note past the 33rd.

Today, Michael Omartian is a top pop record producer with many Grammy and Dove Awards. My handwriting is still on his Union card.

CHAPTER 6

Our last song together

BY NEIL SEDAKA

RECORDED BY PRATT & McCLAIN ON ABC DUNHILL RECORDS

This will be our last song together

Words will only make us cry

This will be our last song together

There's no other way we can say good-bye

Susanne

Only in hindsight did we realize how our contract with
Anita Kerr would make our dream band come to life.
In one year we each made $70,000 — suddenly, we had
the money to finance the vision.

Our elation, however, didn't come until after our
last engagement. We opened for Johnny Mathis in
December 1969 through to New Year's Eve. We drove
down Sunset Blvd. with mixed emotions as we stared
at the advertising billboard picturing our group, The
American Scene, beside Mathis. For four years we'd
been a close-knit cluster of friends. Our haphazard start
turned into a star-studded dream world. We had done
television shows, recorded with major companies, had
performed with superstars, and had seen more of the
country than most kids ever dreamed about. And just a
month earlier we had been asked by the State
Department to represent the U.S. and sing for our
troops in Okinawa, Japan, Thailand and the Philippines.

Jerry and I, though, were the only ones still eager
to stay in the entertainment business. The rest were

making other plans. I guess that's why our farewell performances left me so sentimental. This would be our last song together.

Our kind heavenly Father must have noticed my blues because amidst them He beamed down a ray of hope for the future.

After our act, Johnny Mathis, gracious star that he is, brought us back on stage to sing with him.

The song he chose was a favorite gospel tune written by Neil Diamond. The first line perfectly described what we were dreaming of: "Brother Love, say... Brother Love's, traveling' salvation show..." On stage, Jerry and I looked and pointed at each other. It was the perfect name for our new group.

So, Brother Love we became. Jerry opened a bank account, deposited our new earnings and away we went. Then we began to put the show together in our small apartment.

Michael Omartian came over and we circled him at the keyboard. The magic of Michael was that he not only captured our ideas but instantly expanded on them.

Jerry told Michael that with him at the keyboard, the stage would already be overflowing with talent. Michael shied from the compliment and told us frankly that though he was anxious to get us started, he didn't know how long he could travel with us on the road. Opportunities were arising for him in L.A. He recommended a talented singer presently touring with the Continentals but looking for an opportunity to advance his career. We knew we had a treasure when the

blonde shag-haired Texan auditioned. Truett Pratt's
voice was confident and pleasant — and so was he.

Jerry and I felt we were living out our destinies. At
rehearsals we started with a prayer and then the ideas
popped out like popcorn. We wanted to continue to
keep the pace fast and fun. But, now, instead of just
being clean-cut, the songs would lead into a message.

We decided to open every show with the "Brother
Love" song, then highlight each singer using songs with
positive lyrics written by contemporary songwriters
like Elton John, Ann Murray, and the Carpenters.

We revised our Roaring '20s routine and used it as
a stepping stone for a flashback in time, imagining how
the stars of the '30s, '40s and '50s would have sung the
songs of today. Truett impersonated Rudy Vallee war-
bling "Midnight Cowboy," Diane and I imitated The
Modernaires smoothing out "Something in the Way She
Moves," and Jerry pretended to be like "the Drifters,
sifters and hubcap stealers" of the '50s singing "Let the
Sun Shine In."

We settled on "Learning to Live Together" as lead-in
to Jerry's solo "Garden of Gethsemene" taken from the
rock opera, "Jesus Christ Superstar." We would sandwich the gospel message between those two songs.

The act got better and better with each rehearsal
and our excitement mounted.

Diane and I sought out designers for new cos-
tumes. We wanted to look different — so we would
stand out (a tip we learned from Sonny Bono long ago).
We outfitted the guys in white suits with snakeskin

print shirts. Our blouses had the same print and we were fitted with white jumpers and bell bottom pants that we shed half-way through the show. We also made the most of the popular look of red, white, and blue. We picked out American Flag ties for the guys and tri-colored mini-skirt outfits for us.

After five months, we were ready. Jerry felt we needed a personal manager to add credibility, so we went into a studio and taped a 25-minute show. We sang and Michael played all the instruments (tracking is an amazing convenience).

Jerry called Jim Fitzgerald, a manager with an impressive reputation. Mr. Fitzgerald said "no" at first. Jerry, as usual, relentlessly pursued him until Mr. Fitzgerald agreed to watch us audition at a rented Hollywood studio. Our fresh start now teetered on this manager's approval. Thumbs up: we were on our way. Thumbs down: what would Jerry pull out of his hat then?

My nervous fingers fumbled as I tried to button my costume that morning. It took concentrated effort to get it right. Jerry, on the other hand, breezed into the studio like he owned the place.

We set up and when everything was ready Jerry urged us on, "Let's show him how good we are." He pivoted and flashed a smile. "Mr. Fitzgerald, we've put together a show that will knock your socks off. I've gathered around me some of the finest talent performing today. We hope it's what you're looking for."

Jerry turned back to face us. "One, two, three…"

And we were off. "Brother love, say brother love's,

traveling salvation show…"

I poured on the charm. Halfway through I noticed Mr. Fitzgerald's excitement about our show. He was smiling and tapping his toes. We had him hooked.

As we ended, Mr. Fitzgerald jumped to his feet.

"That's great," he said. "I love it. I can see you playing in concerts, in nightclubs, on television. In fact, you'd be a great for everything. Hey! I need to get busy."

We all laughed and blew out a breath of relief.

Jerry then auditioned musicians for the band. We hired a drummer, guitarist, and keyboard player. No more voting. Jerry plainly told them his criteria: no drugs, no affairs. And he looked for hearts as eager as ours to reach out with the gospel.

Packing for our first engagement, I hummed the gospel song, "O Happy Day."

Jerry came from behind and wrapped his arms around me. "It is one of my happiest days," he said.

Then he remembered he needed to pack his razor. Over his shoulder he called, "Hey you blonde bombshell, don't forget to pack your bikini and tennis racquet."

I played along. "In Seattle? Don't you think a raincoat and umbrella would be more like it?"

"Oh no, Baby. It's going to be sunny and warm. We'll play tennis every day and if you can't beat me at least you can distract me."

"Oh Jerry." Yet to myself I whispered, "Dear Lord, let it always stay this way."

CHAPTER 7

Brother Love's Traveling Salvation Show

BY NEIL DIAMOND

PERFORMED WITH JOHNNY MATHIS

Brother Love, say Brother Love's

Traveling Salvation Show

Pack up the babies and grab the old ladies

And everyone goes, 'cause everyone knows

It's Brother Love's Show

I looked out over the audience in the plush Seattle hotel lounge. It was our first engagement: time to test the waters. Tonight I would tell a night club audience that our happiness was genuine and we had Someone to thank for it.

I stepped back as Susanne sang her soulful "You've Got a Friend." My heart was beating so hard I was afraid the mike would pick it up.

Then I noticed a man across the room. He looked like a businessman, his white dress shirt taut across his chest, his attention riveted on our performance. His face relaxed when our eyes met. It was as if he was saying to me, "I'm glad you're for real. I've had my fill of phonies."

The next song skipped to a key higher and, singing out, I turned to the other side of the semi-circle of faces and saw a young woman. She looked at me with the same earnestness. "Sing it like it is," she seemed to tell me.

My eyes jumped to the table next to her. A slim, balding man locked his eyes on me, too.

After our banjo medley, Truett began, "Learning to live together..." He moved with the beat and held the mike high as he hit the notes strong. Then the music slowed and that was my cue. This was the chance I'd been waiting for — time to tell them what we were about.

"If we went around the room here at the Trojan Horse and asked you what you thought of the idea of learning to live together, I'm sure everyone would say it's a beautiful idea.

"But as we travel across the country, we find people across our broad land have failed at learning to live together. So, we, as Brother Love, decided to use music to share an idea: the reason we're not learning to live together is because we're spiritually divided.

"There's a rock opera touring the country called 'Jesus Christ Superstar.' It's about the one Man who can stop our spiritual division. So, tonight, with your kind permission, I ask that you journey with me 2,000 years ago, kneel very low beneath the bushes at the Garden of Gethsemane, and see the humanity and the godliness of Jesus as He reaches out to the Father for inspiration."

I closed my eyes and gave them my heart. "I only want to say, if there is a way, take this cup from me...."

I suspended the last note, then dropped my head. I kept it down, collecting myself and heard the applause start. It spread across the room in seconds and grew into a roar. I looked up and people were standing. A brunette at the closest table brushed away a tear.

Now was the time to put the offer out there.

Truett smiled at the audience and said it gently.

"We have one more song before we go. If we left you with a lot of music and a few good laughs, it would be an okay show. But we have something more we'd like to share with you — something of ourselves. We want to tell you what makes Brother Love tick.

"You see, we've all found happiness. Now, that might not sound like much, until you think of all the agony and disappointment you can experience in a lifetime — years and years of not knowing what tomorrow will bring. Those of us in Brother Love don't have to worry about that. And the reason we don't worry can be summed up in one word, the name of our next song — "Lord." This is the prayer of our hearts — the seven of us on stage — and maybe it will be your prayer, too.

Truett began:

> *"Lord, if you could only listen*
> *And hear the confusion in my mind*
> *You'd break down and you'd cry for me*
> *You'd break down and you'd die for me*

I stepped up to the mike:

> *Now listen, Lord, you know the feelin'*
> *The feelin' that I've let you down*
> *And Lord, would you break down and cry for me*
> *Lord, would you break down and die for me*

The girls joined us:

> *And Lord, to live from day to day*
> *Will never help me find the way*
> Diane and Susanne sang in harmony:
> *Lord, will you take my hand*
> *Lead me there, to your side, forever, my Lord*

The band picked up the beat and I gave our farewell. "Thanks for coming out tonight. We'll be here at the Trojan Horse for the next four weeks. So we hope to see you again. And, say, if anyone would like to talk to us after the show, we'll be hanging around for a while. Good night everybody."

We swept into our theme song, "Brother Love, say Brother Love's travelin' salvation show...."

Later, Susanne and I said elated good-nights to the band and closed the motel room door. She twirled about.

"It's working, it's really working..." she sang.

Just like the vision I told Hal about, we were reaching out with the gospel in a nightclub.

Susanne couldn't get over it. She paced the room. "We were telling them about Jesus and...it's like... they're looking for the way just like I was..."

I laughed and grabbing her by the waist. "Isn't it great?" I pulled her close. She was breathing hard; suddenly so was I.

"This is just the start, Honey. There's so many we can reach this way." My eyes searched hers. Then I smiled, slowly. "And I don't think the Lord would mind if we had some fun while we're at it."

"Oh, it's that kind of fun you have in mind," she twinkled.

"Well, after eyeing the prettiest girl in the place all night, you've got me all turned on."

Susanne chuckled deep in her throat. I leaned over to kiss her neck, but she pulled away. I ran after her. "Come here, you're driving me crazy."

Later that night, with Susanne asleep by my side, I stared into the dark. I couldn't stop smiling. The band's working, our marriage is working, dreams really do come true. This is going to lead to somewhere very good.

It did. The next morning it led a tall, barrel-chested airline pilot to the feet of Jesus. I was sitting by the pool when he introduced himself to me.

"Hi, I'm Lou Warfield. I really liked your show last night."

"Thanks." I offered him a lounge chair beside me.

"Yeah, there's something different about Brother Love. I'll tell you one thing, the message behind the songs you sang is really great."

"Well, Lou, you know, the message is God loves you and has a wonderful plan for your life. Have you ever considered that?"

The pilot shook his head, waiting for me to go on.

"None of us measure up to God's standards. We sin and that separates us from God and His love. But Jesus came and bridged the gap by paying for our sins.

So all we need to do is receive Jesus Christ as Savior and we can know God's love and have His joy in us every day."

I gave it to him straight. "Would you like to receive Jesus?"

I feared he would laugh, call me a fool. "Yes," he said, his eyes pooled with tears. Lou Warfield had heaven on his mind.

"We could go inside and pray," I offered.

"Here's fine." The man wanted to get to business. So there, by the pool, we bowed our heads together in prayer. Lou received Jesus.

The next time we played at the Trojan Horse, Hal and Jan Lindsey surprised us by dropping in. Jan's father was with them. He laughed and enjoyed the show, but turned serious when he met me in the back alcove afterwards. He said he wanted to make things right. With a drink in one hand and holding my hand with his other, he prayed a sinner's prayer with me.

Jan called us a few days later. We didn't know it, but her father was an alcoholic, staunchly against religion. He refused to go to church. But he heard about our show on the radio and went just to have a good time. He left with much more.

When we opened in Valley Forge, Pennsylvania, Glenn and Crystal McGinnis came up and hugged us. They were among a number of people who kept up with our tour schedules over the years and came to see our act, often flying in to be there. But this was Glen and Crystal's first time seeing our new Brother Love show. Their bear hugs and sincere emotions told us how much they meant it when they said they were touched by the message of Brother Love.

Newspaper reviews were just as encouraging.

"The Brother Love Traveling Salvation Show set up camp this week at the Trojan Horse with the guarantee that they'll save a lot of souls from boredom," reported the *Seattle Post-Intelligencer*. "From their upbeat opening to the closing number, Brother Love fills the stage with such a staggering amount of talent and pleasure that you're almost too stunned to react. But the audiences react — Wow — how they react!"

In upstate New York a reporter wrote, "They prove that entertainment doesn't have to be smutty to be good" *(Syracuse Herald-American)*.

New Orleans received us as well. "Brother Love, currently appearing in the River Queen Lounge at the Marriot Hotel, are dedicated members of the Jesus movement…'Amazing Grace' in a nightclub? Absolutely, and the patrons went for it in an enthusiastic way. They also took Jerry's suggestion and turned to one another and said, 'Hi, glad to meet you'" *(New Orleans The States-Item)*.

Philadelphia Enquirer: "Polished arrangements, talented performers…the audience gave them a standing ovation."

And back in Seattle, the producer for Channel 5 — KING-TV — asked if he could tape our show and broadcast it locally. We shook hands on the deal and he added, "Just be sure to do that 'Jesus thing' at the end."

At age five we lived just 30 minutes away from each other in Van Nuys and Pasadena. On weekends we both went to Griffith Park and rode the ponies. We could have even been there on the same day!

While Susanne and twin sister Diane were starting a musical career singing "Chattanooga Choo Choo" on a local television show, Jerry was busy pitching in Little League at eleven years old.

By 19, the Roshay twins were crowned Twin Queens of the Los Angeles County Fair — sharing the crown, a new car, clothes and boyfriends.

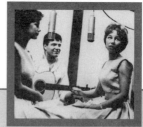

Nick Venet signed the twins to KEEN Records and changed their names to "Dee and Di." They recorded songs they wrote and he later went on to produce Diana Ross. He sure had a great ear for finding new talent!

We graduated from the college campus to the television studios at ABC, where we were semi-regulars on the #1 teen dance show "Shivaree."

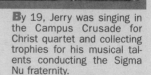

By 19, Jerry was singing in the Campus Crusade for Christ quartet and collecting trophies for his musical talents conducting the Sigma Nu fraternity.

Here is where it all began! Our group called, Somebody-Anybody-Everybody, won the Sweepstakes in UCLA's Spring Sing at the Hollywood Bowl under the critical eyes of celebrity judges Randy Sparks, Carl Reiner and Leonard Bernstein. From left to right: Dave Fractman, Terry Smith, Diane Roshay, Jerry McCaskill, Chuck Stokes, Susanne Roshay and Jerry McClain.

Just a few years earlier we were singing "Dream" at our high school dances, and now we were singing with the Everly Brothers in person.

Dean Martin's producer Greg Garrison caught our act in Las Vegas and signed us to the Dean Martin Show — our first network television appearance. We sang "C'mon Get Happy." As you can see Dean was already a little "too happy."

Maybe it should say "Un-Lively Set!"

After changing our names to The Lively Set and adding Kenny Ballard, we landed our first big nightclub show — opening for stars Rowen and Martin of television's Laugh-In, at the Riviera Hotel in Las Vegas.

1966 — **W**hat a memorable summer! We were regulars on Kraft Summer Music Hall with new upcoming star and host John "Dimples" Davidson.

George Carlin and Richard Pryor kept the whole cast in stitches every day at rehearsals, so it was no surprise to us that they became big comedy stars.

Susannne went from cheek to cheek with Jerry to nose to nose with the great Jimmy Durante.

We asked Phyillis Diller for marital advice in between shows at Disneyland, and she said "Don't do it!" Too late Phyllis, we're already hitched.

Rev. Hal Lindsey pronounced us man and wife on August 10, 1968 and gave us a word of prophecy — "this marriage will be filled with 'Happy Days'."

The twins joined the Lennon Sisters for a song and Jerry harmonized with the Four Freshmen when we performed at Disneyland.

We shared the stage with Vic Damone as his special guests at the Frontier Hotel in Las Vegas, where we spent our two-day honeymoon. Then we hurried back to perform at Disneyland.

It was "wunnerful wunnerful" working with Lawrence Welk. But he thought our hem lines were not "wunnerful" and it nearly cost us the television show.

We watched John's career fly higher than a "Jet Plane"— and hosted a party for him after his opening night at the Greek Theater.

John "Deutchendorf" became a close friend and even serenaded us in our first honeymoon home. John "Denver" became a big star, but he remains very special to us.

"Chances Are" there could not have been a better way to end 1969 than to perform our last song together as The American Scene with the great and talented Johnny Mathis.

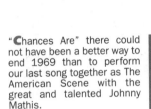

Television's Bat Masterson (Gene Barry) needed some talented young performers in his Las Vegas show. We were glad to oblige...Podner!

The Lively Set became The American Scene for one year as producer Anita Kerr directed us in commercials for American and Standard Oil and recordings with Dot Records.

A new year — a new group! "Brother Love," with new members Truett Pratt and keyboard genius Michael Omartian, takes its travellin' salvation show on the road.

While performing in Seattle, we added new band members Bill Hill and Dave Swanson and joined Hal Lindsey on stage to sing at many of his crusades and on television shows. Jerry "preaches" to Hal and Jan during one of our shows at the Trojan Horse.

No "blues" for us as we sing with the awesome B.B. King in Las Vegas at the Tropicana Hotel. The boys in the band jammed with B.B. after hours and picked up a few new chords. (Barney Robertson, Bob Walden and Dave Herring)

Sandi Miller replaces Diane (who chose matrimony over stardom) and we introduce Sandi to our manager Jim Fitzgerald, joined here by his talented wife Jane Powell at our opening night in Miami Beach.

Susanne and Sandi harmonized with Second Chapter of Acts sisters, Annie and Nellie Herring, as they help us sing on one of our early recordings at Columbia Records.

"Sunday...Monday... Happy Days!" Truett, Michael and Jerry in the recording studio making a hit record.

Overnight success finally after 10 years! "Happy Days" the #1 television show in the country led to our big break. We recorded our first hit record for Warner Bros. Records.

Our band acquired some new members and we had fun singing "Happy Days" all across the country. Clowning around are left to right: Dave Swanson, Lynn Coulter, Carmen Swanson, Truett Pratt, Rod Schaub, Susanne and Jerry.

Opening Cahoots Cabaret at the Sheraton Valley Forge for the Bicentennial Celebration with President Ford.

Jerry acting crazy on TV with superstar Dick Van Dyke.

The Midnight Special with Wolfman Jack, Natalie Cole, Captain and Tennillle and Chuck Berry was indeed special.

Ed McMahon says... "Heeeere's Jerry!"

In Las Vegas with Merv Griffin.

Jerry teaches Mike Douglas to sing "Happy Days" as James Bond (Roger Moore), Vanessa Redgrave and Happy Days' Donny Most look on.

Nothing could be finer than to sing "Happy Days" with Dinah"... Shore that is, on her TV show.

Singing "Happy Days" never gets old, and neither does Dick Clark.

A dream come true: singing "Happy Days" on American Bandstand, a American tradition.

Jerry co-hosts "Dialing for Dollars" TV show.

We first met Jim Stafford during the early days at the Clearwater Hilton in Florida. Years later we're both singing our hits on The Smothers Brothers Show.

From American Bandstand to high school grandstand, Jerry spent many happy days teaching his son Jarret at Alemany High School.

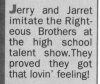

Jerry and Jarret imitate the Righteous Brothers at the high school talent show. They proved they got that lovin' feeling!

Father and son entertaining students at Homecoming activities.

Pepperdine student-director Jarret goes over script changes with his dad for the TV show. Remember, son: dad always has The Last Word!

From Hollywood to Nashville's Dove awards at the Grand Ole Opry and a chance to visit backstage with Amy Grant, one of the most gracious talents we have ever met.

Jarret puts on his first tuxedo as we attend the Grammy Awards Show with the Omartians.

Mike and Stormie Omartian, Paul Johnson and family and Donna Summer join us at the American Cinema Awards show honoring Elizabeth Taylor and Michael Jackson.

Since we are never at a loss for words, hosting our own radio talk show is a natural for us.

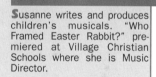

Susanne writes and produces children's musicals. "Who Framed Easter Rabbit?" premiered at Village Christian Schools where she is Music Director.

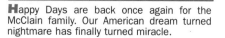

20 years later, jukeboxes and video kareokes all over the world are still playing "Happy Days."

Happy Days are back once again for the McClain family. Our American dream turned nightmare has finally turned miracle.

CHAPTER 8

Hallelujah child

BY JERRY McCLAIN

Hallelujah child, Hallelujah woman

Hallelujah child, Hallelujah woman

Yesterday I tried to write a song

About my wife and little baby son

All I really, really wanted to say is

How much I love you both this beautiful day

Susanne

After singing with Diane all my life, I couldn't imagine singing without her. But she made a quick exit when a better offer came along.

His name: Ed Finnegan.

We were back at the Seattle Trojan Horse six months after our first show, this time, though, with lots of local fans. People pressed the walls, brought by friends to see us. Ed Finnegan's sister had seen us and dragged him in on crutches, recovering from a broken leg.

The magic, as Diane and Ed like to call it, happened between shows. Ed, burly and good-looking, lumbered up to me and paid our band a compliment. Then he pointed across the room.

"Boy, is that brunette cute! I'd sure like to meet her if she's not going with anybody."

I know it sounds like a typical Hollywood movie, but their eyes and hearts locked and they were an instant item. Ed followed us to our next date in Stockton, California. After the show, he pulled Diane to a side table.

"I'm crazy about you," he told my enraptured sister. "I'm afraid if I let you go, I'll never see you again. Will you marry me and move up to Seattle?"

"Yes," she said.

As quick as that, she was gone to make wedding plans. How could she say yes so quickly when it took me four years?

Of course, I was happy for her. But it put us in a predicament. Who could we find to replace Diane?

I turned the worry into a prayer and suddenly Michael Omartian's girlfriend, Sandi Miller came to mind. She had ideal qualifications. The cute Texan brunette sang soprano — as Diane did.

She was a slim 5'1", the same as Diane. She'd fit into all Diane's designer stage clothes.

Best of all, Sandi had six years of performing experience with Campus Crusade's New Folk Singers. (She was also the bubbliest Christian I knew.)

So Sandi replaced Diane and we were back on the touring trail.

Except Sandi was more than we bargained for.

She showed up ready for the road — with 27 pieces of luggage. She packed like flamboyant Liz Taylor.

"Which ones *must* you take?" Jerry asked her, standing behind the van with the rear doors open.

"All of them," she insisted.

Jerry had a private talk with her, which he repeated many times over the years, about her attachment to excess baggage.

The airport authorities also talked to her — sternly. She was lugging a new bag and I asked her what was in it.

"The solution to every medical problem," she said.

When the bag went under the surveillance x-ray, an officer pulled her aside.

"Ma'am, what do you have in that bag?" he demanded.

"Vitamins," she said brightly.

"Nobody carries that many vitamins." The officer contradicted.

"Really…Sir." Manners were lost on this guy. He figured he knew a drug trafficker when he saw one.

"See, this one makes your nails strong and this one," she pointed at the bottom row, "clears your skin."

The officer nodded and smirked. "Right. I'll just hold onto these for you."

We tried not to laugh as she waved good-bye to her $100 health store investment.

We knew Sandi was no convict — she was more of a comic. Her perfect match would have been Mr. Magoo. They had so much in common.

One night she was running late, as usual, and dashed on stage without looking herself over. We sang the opening, danced around while Jerry and Truett introduced us, then began our rendition of Roaring '20s songs. During the number I glanced down and saw she was wearing one red boot and one blue one.

Then there were her idiosyncrasies. "Have you seen my sunglasses?" she asked every day. After awhile we just patted our heads, sign-language, because that's where her sunglasses always were — on top of her head. She even wore them like that at night.

Although her glasses seemed attached, part of her head was, in fact, removable. We wore wigs — or falls, as they are now called — to give managed fullness. Once, in Cincinnati, however, Sandi didn't have time to manage hers so well. Hurried, as usual, she stuck two pins in it and went on stage with a glittering smile.

During one of the fast maneuvers in our choreography, Sandi ducked under Truett's banjo.

She made it under — her fall didn't. It hung, suspended from the banjo pegs, spinning in the air.

Then there was the night in Hawaii when her forgetfulness nearly got us a scandalous review. She just couldn't get a pesky false eyelash to stay on and the band was already playing the lead-in number. One eye looked half the size as the other.

"Come as quick as you can," I sympathized.

The band improvised as long as they could. Finally, Jerry signaled for us to begin. As he took the mike, Sandi suddenly appeared, eyelash in place. The band whistled. Why the sudden gawking?

I looked over and gasped. "Oh my gosh, Sandi, you forgot your hot pants!"

She couldn't hear me over the noise and looked puzzled. Jerry and Truett turned and saw what I did. Her mini-skirt, like mine, had a split up the middle and where hot pants were supposed to be — Sandi displayed nothing but flesh-colored stockings. They, too, attempted to tell her but their poorly suppressed laughter made their words come out in gasps.

She turned to face the audience, still unaware.

Eyes bugged and hands covered open mouths. This was not the show they expected.

"You're Always Well-dressed in Hanes and a Smile," the ad said. Sandi wore both, but not much else.

Her heart was in the right place, though. She always stayed after the show to talk with the audience. Wherever we played, she made close friends. One evening three stewardesses poured their hearts out to her into the morning hours. They wanted answers to end the confusion in their lives. Sandi shared with them the Answer she'd found. Jesus became the Answer for Janet Pyle, Jan McGeary and Cecie Doucet, too.

Sandi made road life bearable for me. She became my new "sister" and I loved her. Jerry got up early in the morning, no matter how late the show went the night before, and started calling or visiting radio stations and booking new dates. In the afternoon, he and the guys headed for the gym to work out or play racquetball. I would have been a stranded motel-wife if not for Sandi.

We'd hit the shops, then find a quaint café to sit and share a laugh, or just relax by the pool. Life was sweet then: I had the Lord in my heart, a happy marriage and a kindred spirit to share my days with.

Jerry loved Sandi like a sister, too. He respected her firm convictions and the way she gently led so many to the Lord.

It seemed natural to have her come live with us when we found our house. Or should I say when *I* found our house. One day I looked out the window of our apartment just off the UCLA campus and decided it was time to move to a more pleasant location.

"This is summer in California," I complained to Jerry. "So, where's the sun?" Every day at four in the afternoon, a depressing fog rolled in. Yet, Jerry wasn't convinced life could ever be lived far from the UCLA campus. (He was accumulating blue and gold clothing like a model trying to start a new trend.)

But I looked out at the fog and remembered my school days in nearby San Fernando Valley. It had the perfect weather combination: sunny with a constant breeze.

Jerry and I made a deal. For a week, he would try to find a house in Westwood, by the campus, and I would search in the San Fernando Valley. Whoever found a dream house came out the winner.

The Valley is made up of 10 small cities, actually. The one I liked the best was Toluca Lake near Universal Studios: serene streets, well-kept lawns, thick, overlapping ivy twirled up trees and fences. Flowers bloomed along winding walkways.

My third day out, I turned onto Auckland Avenue and spotted a "For Lease" sign. It was posted in front of a small yellow stucco house, skirted with brick and a white picket fence. The owners gladly showed me around.

As I stepped into the living room I was charmed; an open-ended fireplace connected the living room with the den on the other side, a step below. To my right was the square dining room which attached to a galley kitchen. Out the kitchen door, a remodeled garage included a small apartment. (What a perfect office for Jerry.) A screened-in porch, attached to the back end of the house, added another room, considering the constant breeze.

Jerry didn't have such luck, so I won the bargain.

We gave Sandi the second bedroom. It didn't make sense for her to pay rent somewhere when we spent weeks at a time on the road.

With Sandi came a lot of fur and fluff — she had a fetish for stuffed animals. She even took them on the road; no doubt they took up one or two of her 27 suitcases. Hoping to encourage her to leave the bunnies and bears at home, we gave a silent nod to her request to decorate her room in early Winnie-the-Pooh.

We even left it that way when Sandi decided to leave the band after two years for a job with Continental Airlines. The room's new occupant would love it, we were sure, because I was pregnant.

At the same time Sandi broke the news that she was leaving the show, Cliff "Barney" Robertson, our keyboard player, was offered a job playing with country singer Waylon Jennings. Suddenly we needed crucial replacements.

Jerry rang Campus Crusade Headquarters and talked with Bob Horner, leader of The New Folk.

"In your travels, I thought you might have run across some talent you could turn me on to," Jerry explained. "I'm looking for a couple, a guy who plays piano and a gal who can sing."

Bob did have a lead. He suggested a black couple he met while The New Folk were in Portland, Oregon. "They sang a lovely duet together and he played piano. They were great."

"Do you remember their names?"

"No I don't. But they were members of the church there. I'll call the pastor and find out."

They were Dave and Carmen Swanson, and Jerry located them in Chicago.

He called Dave. "My name is Jerry McClain," he said. "I have a band called Brother Love and I need a keyboard player and a girl singer. Bob Horner of Campus Crusade saw you perform and I'd like to hire you. We open in New Orleans in one month. Would you like to join us?"

I thought the guy would hang up on Jerry, but suddenly a smile spread across my husband's face.

Dave said, "We've been praying that God would deliver us from Chicago. We hate it here. We'd love to come, but we're so broke we don't have enough money for gas to get back to California."

Jerry sent them a credit card. They joined us in time for two weeks of rehearsal before we opened in New Orleans.

The first time I met Carmen I was awed by her striking beauty. Then I heard her sing. After she finished, I walked up to her, face to face.

"Listen," I said. "I've been in the entertainment business my entire life. I see I'm going to have to set

down a new rule: either you can look beautiful on
stage or you can have an incredible voice. But I don't
think I can deal with both at the same time. You need
to either mess up your face or do something to your
voice."

Carmen laughed, but did neither. She went out
and stunned everybody. We became instant friends and
she taught me how to play the gospel tambourine.

Dave was just as incredible. One of our newer acts
was an Oldies Rock & Roll Show. But when Barney left
we thought we might have to drop it. Barney could
improvise easily when we spontaneously used requests
from the audience to make up a medley of favorites.
And we pulled up volunteers to join us as back-up
singers. We doubted a replacement would have that
versatility.

But we soon found out Dave could not only impro-
vise...he was also a terrific singer. He added a Nat King
Cole Medley (including "Blueberry Hill" and "Ramblin'
Rose") and melted hearts (notably Carmen's) with Sam
Cook's "You Send Me."

Our new band was complete. Bill Hill from
Alabama played drums and impersonated John Wayne
while Zavier played both rock and classical guitar with
equal ease.

I stayed with the band until I was seven months
along. I was glad to be home, nesting. I fixed up the
nursery, finding places for all the wonderful gifts I
received at the three baby showers given in my honor.
I shopped and cleaned, visited friends, cooked Jerry a

string of square meals, then shopped and cleaned some more. I was tired of the road and ready to settle down.

One day in my eighth month I went to Jerry frantic, fearing the worst. I couldn't feel the baby move.

We rushed to Dr. Van ver Ahe's office. He attached a fetal monitor and reassured us that the baby was fine. Jerry was ecstatic when he heard the heart beat. He decided we were going to have a girl because the baby's heart rate was 152. (He read somewhere that anything above 140 meant a girl.)

The due date came and went without a sneeze from our little bambino. The doctor reconsidered delivery and recommended a C-section, citing the difference between the baby's head and my small frame. He told me to pick the date: the day before Thanksgiving or the day after. Since I wasn't about to eat a hospital version of a Thanksgiving meal, I emphatically told him it would be the day after.

I checked into the hospital Thanksgiving night with a queen's entourage. I had my bags, my husband, two sets of in-laws, Truett and his wife Linda, more relatives, more friends — 20 well-wishers in all came to herald our baby's passage into the open air.

A nurse attached a fetal monitor and told us the heart beat was 160. Jerry kissed me good-bye and promised me pink roses. That night he and the band performed at a local club. When he got home at 2:30 in the morning he sat at the electric keyboard and tried to write a song for our soon-to-arrive Shannon Lee.

Nothing would come. He stayed up until it was

time to meet me at the hospital for the C-section, but he couldn't think of a rhyme or a set of notes worth remembering. I was drowsy when he told me his frustration, "Here's the biggest event of our lives and I can't think of a tune to save my soul."

And was Jerry ever surprised when the doctor announced the baby's birth — we named him Jarret Kent.

When Jerry brought us home, the rocking chair was sitting beside a blazing fire. Jerry said he wanted to sing us the song he received the night of Jarret's birth. While I was recovering in the hospital, Michael Omartian pitched in and recorded a beautiful accompaniment for it. As Jarret and I sat in our place, Jerry pushed the tape player to start the music.

I tried to look completely domestic and serene, holding my bundle of joy, but baby Jarret was not happy with his new surroundings. I smiled weakly to Jerry as he sang:

> *"I know it's hard to put in a few lines*
> *All the memories that's gone down,*
> > *the good times*
> *But I'm trying very hard, the best I can*
> *To say thanks for the son, I love you, Susanne."*

As Jerry sang, I tried to calm Jarret so I could appreciate this tender moment. There had to be a trick to how nurses wrap these blankets, I thought. I was worried the fire was too hot for the baby, but when I tried to unwrap him he nearly spun to the floor.

Jerry, oblivious to my struggle, finished with:

> *Hallelujah child, hallelujah woman*
> *Hallelujah child, hallelujah woman*
> *Yesterday I tried to write a song*
> *About my wife and little baby son*
> *All I really, really wanted to say is*
> *How much I love you both this beautiful day.*

Jerry's face glistened with tears. He appeared as sentimental as I'd ever seen him. I was crying too — but not from sentiment. I couldn't figure out how to make this pint-sized red head stop wailing in my ear.

Our work lives forever separated after the baby came. Jerry went touring without me, while I sat home waiting for Jarret's new teeth to come in. Jerry came home exhausted from socializing; I was exhausted from not socializing. (Jarret slept like a musician, was up all night, catnaps all day.)

"This is not New Orleans," I told the mixed up sleeper, blurry-eyed. "We can't go on this way."

He finally got turned around after his first year and Jerry and I had this new "little love" in common. We both delighted in sitting on the floor with our freckled fixation, hearing him jabber a story to us. Jerry told him he was going to be a great baseball player some day and I told him that with lungs like he had he was headed for the opera. I dressed him up in denim with rhinestones and we showed him off as I got back in costume and sang with the band.

Jerry and I rolled on the floor with Jarret, applauded his toilet training efforts, and were awed when he put out his own place mat. Like always, we resembled Dorothy and friends in my favorite movie *The Wizard of Oz*. We journeyed through life singing a happy song.

But then we came to a bend in the road and we didn't see the dangers. If only Jerry had not stopped to sniff those poisonous poppies.

CHAPTER 9

We had it all

BY T. SEALS AND D. FRITTS

RECORDED BY JERRY McCLAIN ON ABC DUNHILL RECORDS

Remember how I used to touch your hair

While reaching for the feeling

That was always there

You were the best thing in my life

I can recall

You and me, Lord knows, we had it all

The record business is a funny thing. Most of the work goes on behind the scenes, so it looks like magic when a song is suddenly #1 on the charts. I realized that if I was ever going to have a hit record, I needed to find out what was behind the magic.

We had just signed on with ABC/Dunhill to do an album, "Pratt & McClain," and I wasn't about to sink heart and soul into another recording only to be told afterwards, "Nice try, boys. But it just won't sell."

It had happened to us too many times already. We made records as The Lively Set, The American Scene, and our latest, with Columbia Records, as Brother Love. A few records sold — the ones we bought.

"What are we doing wrong?" I asked Dennis Laventhal, seated in his office. He was vice-president of promotions for ABC/Dunhill.

He put his elbows on his desk. "It's the way the record is sold," Dennis said. "It's the little local stations that add up to make a song popular. Oh sure, record companies thank the big city stations because they represent millions of listeners. But the big city boys play what's popular with the little stations."

I did some fast thinking. I could get out there and meet the small station DJs.

I immediately started dialing, setting up a road trip. My fingers drummed the desk as I waited for the operator. "I'm going to get to know these guys," I said aloud to myself, "and see what makes this record business work."

I was gone for a month. I shook hands in Columbus, Ohio, interviewed live in Boise, Idaho, even went home and met a DJ's family in Shreveport, Louisiana. Dennis was right — they did have their fingers on the pulse of the public.

And they were glad I stopped by. Appreciation from big stars was scarce; my gratitude was a refreshing contrast.

"Wanna catch a bite to eat after this?" I'd offer. Over lunch they taught me the in's and out's of reporting what their listeners liked. We exchanged funny stories and sad ones — their experiences with people over the air waves and mine from the stage. By the end of the month I had 50 new friends and an education.

And I got it just in time.

Michael came over on Tuesday with a song in his hand.

"Ever watch 'Happy Days' on TV? You know, the sit-com?"

"No. I've never seen it." I ushered him and his wife, Stormie, into the den.

"It's climbing the charts, soon to be one of the

most popular shows on television." He waved the sheet music he held. "This is the new theme song for the show. Steve Barri and I were asked to produce it. I want you to sing the lead. It needs a pop sound with a lot of enthusiasm. You're a natural." He looked at Susanne. "In fact, we'll need your whole group."

"When?" I asked eagerly.

"Tomorrow."

I arrived at the studio early and chatted with the musicians. They told me the show was a take-off from a skit on another show called "Love American Style." The skit was so popular, the producers capitalized on the '50s attraction and retained Ron Howard and Anson Williams who played straight-laced Richie Cunningham and his friend Potsie. They later added a motorcycle tough, The Fonz.

"Kids love the show — especially The Fonz." The bald engineer leaned back and did his best Fonzie imitation — thumbs up, "Aaayyh." I shook my head, feeling out of step.

"Jerry, you're on," Michael called. The engineer chuckled behind me.

I walked into the studio, where Truett, Susanne, and the rest of the group were already warming up.

We got to work and in a few takes we had it.

I liked the song. It was clean, vivacious and reminded me of college days when Susie and I were going steady. I winked her way as I sang the second verse, "Gonna cruise her 'round the town, show everybody what I'd found, rock n' rolling with all my friends, hoping the feelin' never ends…"

"Thanks, man." I shook Michael's hand firmly. "I hope it's what you needed."

Michael smiled and shook back. "Jerry, I've got a feeling it's just what you needed."

He was right, as it turned out. Two evenings later, Susanne and I were driving my convertible to a gig in L.A. when we flicked on the radio.

"Sunday, Monday, Happy Days…"

"Hey, that's us!" we said. "They're playing it… they're playing our song!"

With the radio blaring, Susanne and I flew down the L.A. freeway. We laughed and said a million times, "I can't believe it."

We had finally made it to the big time.

Truett was just as excited. Our dream of a hit record was coming true after all these years, and planning our promotion tour was very exciting. Susanne was a little apprehensive about how she would be able to travel, sing, and take Jarret on the road. Our problems were solved when we hired our new drummer, Lynn Coulter, and he brought his wife, Molly, along on tour. She became Jarret's first nanny and they really became part of the Brother Love family.

All stops were pulled. The preceding years of honing my performing skills paid off. I was at home on stage and gave 110% each time we sang the song. We appeared on the Dinah Shore, Mike Douglas and Merv Griffith shows. When Wolfman Jack introduced us on ABC's "Midnight Special" we performed in front of our names in lights three times our size and then shared the stage with Captain and Tennille, Natalie Cole and the legendary Chuck Berry.

My small town radio buddies sent a message of support by reporting requests for "Happy Days" at their stations — even before the record was released! It worked. Starting in April 1976, "Happy Days" was #5 on Billboard's Top 40s chart for 10 weeks.

My hair was longer now and I wore bellbottom jeans studded with rhinestones over platform shoes. Unfortunately, that wasn't all that changed about me. Ten years of watching how people compromised in this business wore me down. It was easier for the record company to just send Truett and me to promote by ourselves without the band, so we dropped the name Brother Love and became just Pratt & McClain. Susanne no longer performed on stage with me, except for a few big performances now and then. As she stayed home with Jarret, we were like two hands missing a clap. I distanced myself from her and was off on my own trip — without her at my side I wasn't held accountable and could do just as I wanted. After all — I deserved this success and I was going to take advantage of it. It didn't help matters that I had given up daily prayer, Bible study, and going to church. Nothing mattered except my career!

You can guess what happened then…I fell flat on my face and began my slow decline.

For instance, there was our debut on "American Bandstand." After we sang "Happy Days," Dick Clark talked to us on national television.

"This wasn't an overnight success for you guys, was it?" he asked.

"No," Truett said. "We've been playing in night clubs and concerts and fairs for years."

Dick turned to me. "I understand you guys work a lot in Las Vegas, Jerry."

"Yeah. We learn a lot about performing there. With so many other entertainers in Las Vegas, it's a great place to work on our act."

"But you can't spend all your time on stage. What do you do in between shows?"

"Oh we go out and we shoot a little craps." (It wasn't true but I thought it sounded "with it.")

I compromised on song selection, too. The second hit from our "Happy Days" album was "Devil with the Blue Dress On." The lyrics bothered me at first. We really could have picked a more wholesome song with an equally-good rock beat.

But, like everything offered me those days, I figured God and I had an understanding: I had already paid my dues — I told others about Him — so a little compromise now wasn't unreasonable.

That thought would derail my dream.

"You sure you don't want to go?" I asked Susanne. It was a year after we recorded "Happy Days" and it was playing on the radio everywhere. Our album, by the same name, was just as popular. I held an invitation, a golden opportunity — one of the many that poured in daily. Warner Bros. was throwing a big bash to celebrate Fleetwood Mac's multi-million-dollar #1 hit, "Rumours." We were invited.

"Big names are going to be there."

Susanne finished brushing her teeth, wiped her mouth with the towel, and gave me her final decision. "No. Jarret has a fever. You go along with Truett and have your fill of all that Hollywood stuff." I didn't like her insinuation, but she softened it with a kiss. "You have a good time."

I wasn't surprised she felt that way. By now we were living two different lifestyles and I didn't know how to get her up to speed. At least she let me enjoy my success. She also made it possible for me to come back to the every-day-ness of Auckland Ave. and get my feet back on the ground.

Truett thumped my stomach when we entered the Warner Bros. suite. Big name faces were everywhere. It was tempting to whisper and point. But we didn't want to look like amateurs. We would show them we were professionals, too.

I stepped forward and introduced myself to the cluster of people before me. I expressed genuine interest in who they were, what they were about, told them a little about myself and moved on. Using that technique, by the end of the first hour I had the party figured out. I knew where I fit in.

This was a quiet affair — almost like a secret was being passed around. The secret came into view when the circle of partyers around me stepped back to include Elton John, Rod Stewart and George Harrison of the Beatles. A bosomy blonde next to Elton John held his drink while he took a rolled-up $100 bill and placed it at a slight angle over a row of white powder on a square plate of glass. He pinched one nostril, sniffed, and pulled his head back and, then switched to the other side.

He was snorting cocaine. He passed it on with a drunken grin. Everyone was trying it. And it was only three people away from me. I couldn't stop staring at the silent ritual. I heard Truett in my right ear.

"Let's try it, just once," he whispered.

I shook off the nagging doubts and smiled. "Yeah. Just one time."

I was instantly in. Elton John smiled directly into my eyes. His manager patted me on the back. Yeah, they'd remember me when the time was right. I was a hit-song-after-hit-song waiting to happen.

Forget the stuffed shirt approach. I wondered why I hadn't loosened up before. This was living. I was "in" with Jesus and cool with these happenin' movers and shakers.

Ah, I decided inwardly, it's a small price to pay. The name of today's game is compromise. Lawrence Welk can stick to his guns as he waltzes his way into history. I'm getting on with the times — getting in touch with my generation.

And touching — physical touching — appeared to be a big part of the scene. All over the room bodies were intertwined. Suddenly, I didn't belong.

Susanne wasn't with me. And if she saw me right then, I doubted she'd feel like touching.

"Wanna beer?" Truett swaggered as he grabbed my shoulder.

"No, I wanna go home, Truett. It's been great, man, but I think we've had enough."

Truett took some convincing, but eventually we weaved our way down the stairs to my car.

As my red convertible veered down Warner Boulevard, the breeze hit Truett's face, taking him even higher.

"That was great, man. That was great," he kept saying.

I kept my thoughts to myself. Great? Maybe. One time. But I better not let it happen again. I was thinking crazy there for a while. Must be what cocaine does to you. I thought I was invincible.

A different sureness convicted me driving home — I had to face Susanne. She'd read it all over me.

But she didn't. That's what made it easier the second time. And the third and the fourth and so on — pretty soon I was doing coke with everyone who was anyone in Hollywood. And Susanne still didn't see it. There was no tell-tale smell and I could act normal when I got home.

I liked it…the high. I felt free as a bird. A liberating boldness shot right through me with that first inhale. I soared.

And I talked. I always did love talking to people.

But when I was high I had all these creative thoughts I felt compelled to express. Maybe that's what was addictive. All my juices flowed. I philosophized about the world one minute and wrote lyrics to songs and poems the next. I was convinced that whatever I attempted while I was high was far superior to what I did when I was sober.

So I kept snorting. I tried to brush aside the disappointed looks of the secretaries at Warner Bros. They stopped asking about my son, stopped asking to see pictures. They knew I had changed. My new friendliness wasn't the kind they liked. Being stoned marks you. You're no longer a giver, but a taker. They saw that.

Coke wasn't free after a year into my regular use. By that time I was snorting every day. Once, when Truett and I were on the road promoting our third hit record — a disco chart maker, "Whachersign" — he came back to our motel room with some "white magic." I couldn't believe how much he had to pay for it. After we snorted it, I sat straight up. I was supposed to bring Jarret a new baseball glove. I checked my wallet: $25. We still had to eat and buy gas the next day. How was I going to tell Susanne why I didn't have enough cash to buy the gift for our little boy?

I chuckled to myself as I imagined telling her, "We put it up our noses, Honey. It's this little white powder. It made us feel real good. Sorry about the glove. Hey, you look so tired. You should try some coke yourself."

She'd lock me out of the house.

So I played the game. I dodged questions, she guessed answers. It became our pattern. I spent money we didn't have, then acted frustrated when bills came. If she said she needed a some new clothes to replace her maternity outfits, I feigned anger.

"You've got all those hit records, Jerry," she'd retort. "It doesn't make sense that we're hurting for money."

"I don't have time for your complaining, I'm building a career," I'd say.

"You don't have time to be much of a father or husband either."

Every couple weeks we'd go at it again. Then the collectors started calling. Things really heated up at home, so I fled to the refuge of the cool night.

I came home one June morning with one thought on my mind: get to my sock drawer and find my stash of Valium. My nerves were raw: I felt like a tangle of live wires. A few pills and I'd feel better, maybe even sleep.

When I twisted the front door handle open, my hand froze. Someone was coming toward me. I strained to see, squinting in the dark. The form loomed nearer.

"Daddy?" A high pitched voice broke the stillness.

I let out my breath. "Oh Jarret, it's just you." I knelt as he rushed into my arms. His flannel pajamas caressed my tense jaw. I carried him back to bed, staying with him until he was peacefully asleep.

It was his look of peace that came back to me when Susanne forced me awake a few hours later.

CHAPTER 10

Who needs it

BY MICHAEL & STORMIE OMARTIAN

RECORDED BY PRATT & McCLAIN ON WARNER BROS. RECORDS

If this is what love is, who needs it

If this is what love is, who wants it

If this is what love is

Who wants it, who needs it

Susanne

"Jerry, wake up. Someone's here!" I scrambled to get on my robe.

It was Truett pounding on the door. I let him in. He pushed past me and stomped straight back to our bedroom. He looked angrier than I'd ever seen him. His face was red, veins protruding. His blonde hair looked white in contrast.

"Party's over, you traitor!" I heard him shout. "I just found out there's a mess of money missing from our business account. You stabbed me in the back, you louse!"

I hurried in behind Truett. Jerry was struggling to sit up in bed, half-awake.

"Truett," I said. "What are you talking about?"

He yanked a magazine from his back pocket and slapped it on the bed, never taking his eyes off Jerry.

"Read this, little lady, then you'll know the real score...what it's all about. Your big man here is in way over his head."

"What...?"

I looked down and read the bold letters on the cover, "HIGH ON COCAINE."

Like an adding machine, I added up how weird Jerry was lately. Depressed, edgy, he made excuses for why he was never around. He'd lost twenty pounds. The few times he went to church with us he couldn't sit still. He got up again and again during the service, whispering that he had to go to the bathroom.

I knew it was odd, but…

…the money! There was a lot of missing money. Jerry kept switching our checking account from one bank to another. Twice already I tried to use my credit cards and they were denied. I was humiliated, but thought, surely, it was just a mix-up. Jerry must have changed accounts and just forgotten to tell me. But was Truett now saying that Jerry was into drugs? That's what all this was about?

I picked up the *TIME Magazine*, afraid of what I'd find. Dread seeped through me as I flipped the glossy pages. The pictures stood out: a rolled-up $100 bill tilted over a mirror with white powder on it. Another was labeled "coca leaves." Another pictured a police officer weighing a white sack.

Then there were photographs of familiar faces: Louise Lasser from the "Mary Hartman, Mary Hartman" sit-com, Keith Richards of the Rolling Stones rock group, and…Richard Pryor.

I looked up at Jerry, my mouth gaping. We both knew Richard had gotten heavier into drugs since we worked with him in the '60s. And just a year ago his addiction made the news. He nearly blew himself up doing what they called "free basing."

I shook my head. Richard and Jerry were opposites. But Truett said....

I needed to hear it from Jerry. "You're like Richard Pryor?" I asked.

"I never free-base like he does," Jerry slowly defended himself. I hung on his words — hoping he'd clear all this up.

"I never free-base like Richard."

I grabbed the dresser for support. Then it was true. I'd been living with a liar. My Jerry was a drug user. How did he do it without my knowing?

Truett's face flushed even redder. "Free base? You don't need to do that. You put so much up your nose every day, you're taking it in just as fast. And you're using my money to pay for it. You're no partner — you're a thief! And I just caught you, you…" he swore, wild with rage. I was afraid he'd attack.

I looked back at Jerry and, unbelievably, he acted oblivious to both of us. He just sat there like he was in a stupor on the bed. Instead of defending himself, he said to Truett, "I never saw you turn down the stuff."

Truett clenched his fist, trying to control himself, then backed out of the room, pointing and waving his finger at Jerry.

"You've got another think coming if you think I'm going to let this go! You owe me, Bub! You owe me big time!"

Truett hammered the floor with each step and slammed the front door.

I whirled back to Jerry. This was a nightmare.

"What have you done? Have you gone crazy?"

"Quiet Susie." Jerry climbed out of bed to hush me.

"The Bordens next door will hear."

"Hear? They probably wonder what took me so long. Everybody else knows you're doing drugs, and I'm the last to know. My God, you're spending all our money on cocaine." My chest heaved. "That's why the credit cards were denied! That's why you've been acting so weird!"

A fury welled up in me. "You're a jerk, that's what you are! You call yourself a Christian?! You're nothing more than a low-down druggie. You stupid fool! You threw it all away. For what? Dope? Jerry, how could you be so stupid? You've ruined our lives!" I wailed.

Jerry patted my shoulder. "Oh, honey, come on. It's not as bad as all that."

I stared up at him in disbelief. He didn't get it. He....

Then it hit me. He was high. Right there in our bedroom. He wasn't even with me. He was tripping out while I was going through hell.

I slapped his hand away and, with my other fist, pounded his chest. "You made me look like a fool!" I gritted my teeth and screamed. "I hate you!" I kicked him in the shin and walked out.

"You'll have to pay something, ma'am. There's no getting around it anymore. You owe about $600 and that's a lot of money. Now, when can you send the first payment?"

The next day I got another call. "Your bank

account is in arrears, Mrs. McClain. We'll have to stop payment on all your checks until it's cleared up."

The next afternoon: "Your husband said he mailed us a payment, but it's been two weeks and we haven't received it. Can you please come down and pay us in cash today?"

The nightmare only got blacker. It wasn't enough that I knew where the money had gone, now I had the crowd of hecklers calling me every day.

Couldn't you at least leave me alone? My brain screamed. I need time — time to think this through. I wished I could go far away.

I dreaded picking up the phone any more. But I sighed with relief when I heard my sister's voice on the other end. I explained the calls I'd been getting and she sympathized with my misery. She said she had an idea that might help. She wanted to fly Jarret and me up to Seattle, at her expense, for a month.

"Mike and Ryan are out of school for summer vacation," she said. "We can go to Lake Washington, relax, and let the boys play."

Be with a normal, loving family again. It was an offer I couldn't refuse. And, once away, tension had less of a grip on me. The boys floated in innertubes on the lake and told stories by the campfire while I bared my soul to my lifetime best friend. Still, my heart constantly ached. It felt so awkward to laugh. But at least we were away from Jerry.

When we finally returned home, the dilemma was there before me once again. What was I going to do?

Then Darlene Honeycutt called. "Do you remember me?" she asked. "We met a couple months ago at Paul and Kathie Lee Johnson's party." A face started to come to mind. She went on. "You were telling me about how you used to entertain and now you're home with your little boy — and he has red hair just like mine."

"Now I remember."

"Well, I thought of you when my boss said she was looking for a new secretary. I work at the Dorothy Day Otis Children's Theatrical Agency, and Dorothy needs someone who has some knowledge of the entertainment business. I thought of you. I don't know if you've considered going back to work, but it's a pretty fun place. And your little boy could even try out for some commercials. His red hair will make him an instant attraction and you said yourself he's not shy."

"I don't know what to say...."

"Just say you'll think it over and call me back as soon as you can. She needs someone to start right away."

I hung up the phone, dazed. This was too good to be true. A job. And it might work out perfectly. Jarret was attending Village Christian School, and he could ride to school with the neighbor boys. I'd be home in time to fix dinner.

What a boost. When I was feeling most alone, other people — strangers almost — were thinking about me. And the new job that came of it boosted me right out of bed each morning. I earned a paycheck, along with fresh vigor and focus. Jerry was still making a mess of everything, but at least I didn't have to stay home all day and live in the misery of it.

I thanked God for hearing me. The agency was a fun place, and Jarret did fine at school. He also did great in commercials. Through the agency, he was the freckled face in advertisements for Robinsons, Milk Mate and Mattel Toys.

Jarret and I now had a way to get on with our lives. But God soon let me know He had more in mind. Jarret's teacher at Village Christian School approached me after their Spring Concert.

We chatted a few minutes, then she asked if I would consider coming to work at the school. They were looking for a new teacher. I was taken aback.

"How did you know I taught?" I asked her.

"Your son told me. He said you'd be perfect here at Village."

I smiled. Even with all the craziness at home, Jarret still only spoke of the good.

But teaching again? After my experience in south-central L.A. I told myself I wouldn't do it again. Maybe that was unfair. This was a Christian school with families involved. Instead of unrestrained violence, I would be respected.

It would also help financially. My parents were paying for Jarret's tuition, but if I worked there I'd only have to pay half.

"There's no harm in applying," I answered brightly.

My interview with the principal felt like it was meant to be. I was hired on the spot to begin the next Fall.

There was a safeness about Village Christian School that I just couldn't put my finger on.

And I was comforted every morning and afternoon driving with Jarret by my side. He chatted incessantly. Listening to his excited, high-pitched voice, I felt beckoned to try for happiness again.

The days flew by. Only at times — unfortunately, inconvenient times — the pain of Jerry's betrayal broke through. One morning I dismissed the class for recess and had to run to the bathroom. The tears wouldn't stop.

Lynda, a teacher in the next room, walked in. I tried to compose myself and wipe my face.

"Please excuse me," I said nervously. Then I caught sight of myself in the mirror. "Oh dear. I can't face my class like this. Mascara all over, blotchy patches. I look terrible."

"It's okay, Susanne," she soothed. "Is it your class? Did something go wrong this morning?"

"Oh no, not the kids. It's my husband," I blurted. Suddenly it was out in the open. I'd kept it to myself so long. How would Lynda react if she knew what was going on? I searched her eyes. They were kind, inquisitive. I blew a breath out. Why was I trying to be so brave? Here stood a true friend and right now I needed one.

But when I tried to talk, only sobs came out. I couldn't control my emotions. I was so tired, so frayed.

"Just let it out, Susanne." Lynda consoled me with her arm around my shoulders. "You'll feel better."

It was several minutes before I could explain. "Jerry's not been home for three days." I blew my nose. "I haven't heard from him. I don't even know if he's dead or alive." Lynda silently shook her head from side to side in sympathy. "He keeps promising he'll quit, but he can't walk away from drugs." She handed me a fresh tissue. I went on. "I can't understand him. He's messed up everything and still he won't stop. When do I give up hoping he'll change and do something about it?"

Lynda stood quietly for a moment, gathering her thoughts before she spoke. "A lot of us here at Village have been through hard times," she finally said. "Probably every one of us would tell you the same thing: God will make a way. It might look hopeless, but God's especially good at turning around hopeless situations.

"And though — you can be sure — I'll be your friend all the way through this, you might consider seeing a professional counselor. Someone who's more qualified to give you advice. A lot of people are helped that way."

She hugged me tight and prayed that God's loving arms would encircle me and I'd feel His love.

After she left, I patted my eyes with the tissue. She's right, I thought. The only way to get through this is to trust God. He provided a job at the talent agency and then here at Village. He's looking out for us. Where else would I get a hug and a prayer during recess?

I knew, though, that guidance from God wouldn't always be easy to recognize. And I wouldn't get to see the whole plan. Just the next step. If I walked the way

He led me, He'd show me yet another step, causing my faith to grow.

As for seeing a counselor like Lynda suggested, I had some reservations. I'd thought of counselors as doctors for the desperate. Come to think of it, though, that's just how I felt. Desperate. I could manage to trust God, but with all the emotions erupting inside me, I needed help sorting them out.

Soon after, I talked with my close friend, Patty Hardy, and she recommended Min Whaley. "You should call her, Susie," Patty said. "She helped me through an ugly time." Patty had been through a blistering divorce. We became close when she was at her worst. I went over to extend my friendship and invited her to church. She met Jesus, and a new Strength helped her through the separation and settlement. She attributes it to salvation and counseling with Min.

Min was a member of our church, Church on the Way, in Van Nuys, California. But it was such a large congregation, I'd never had the occasion to meet her before.

I felt at home with her the instant we met.

"Sit down here, Susanne," Min directed me on my first visit. "I want to know what's on your heart."

I told her everything that had happened. When I was through, our lives hung in the air looking like a brief sketch, when, inside me, what once was a masterpiece now was slashed into shreds. Did Min get the real picture? Did she know the value of what was lost?

"Your marriage used to be one of the rare ones,"

she said. She knew. I relaxed into the chair.

"Now that he's changed, you're not afraid of him, are you?" Min asked.

"No, he's not a violent man. Just a prideful one. That's what keeps him from changing, I think. Pride's pretty powerful when it's all you have to hang on to."

"What about you, Susanne? Are you holding on to pride?"

I didn't understand what she was shooting at. I was the victim here. I wasn't the one who'd made a shambles out of our marriage and wrecked our happy home.

I answered, "I used to be proud of what we had. But now it's just...embarrassing."

"No...I mean, have you let go? You know, forgiven him?"

I'd never connected the two — pride and unforgiveness — before.

"I guess I have. He's trying to keep a job — I give him credit for that..."

Min stopped me by taking my hands in hers. "No, Susanne. Jerry doesn't deserve to be forgiven. We know that. He's done you wrong. You have a right to be angry.

"But if you stay angry, Satan wins all the way around. He'll have your family wrapped around his finger while he sits back laughing, believe me.

"You don't want that. You came to me because you wanted help for your family. And I'm here to give it to you.

"Forgiveness is what you need. Letting go of the anger you feel. It might seem like a bitter pill to swallow, ignoring the obvious, even. But it's not. It's God's kind of unconditional love. Even though Jerry doesn't deserve it, you're going to forgive him. And you'll start to feel a joy and freedom inside you…" she groped for words. "It's how Shadrach, Meshach and Abednego must have felt when the flames consumed everything around them. Yet, they remained untouched. They saw their God stand up for them.

"You can experience the same, starting today, Susanne. Before you leave we'll pray together. And if you forgive Jerry, you'll go away knowing that Satan didn't win this time.

"And each time the hurt starts to smart again, or you're with Jerry, you can refuse to say angry, vengeful things, and know that Satan loses again and again. Hold back the curses and say only blessings. You'll end up the winner. And the Lord will be cheering the loudest of all. He doesn't want another family torn apart, Susanne. Let's pray."

I did feel freer right away. We met six more times and Min was my buoy in a sea of confusion.

I now realize how frightfully angry I was at Jerry. He was a fool and I wanted him to know it. But Min woke me up to the truth. I was angry because I was hurt. And only by forgiving Jerry and no longer belittling and criticizing him, could I help change the course of our family. If I hadn't reached out to Jerry by extending kindness instead of anger, we might not be together today. Our son would have missed knowing the great father Jerry finally turned out to be.

Min's challenge was true. Only by forgiving did I free God's hands to help me. I faced the challenge of my life.

CHAPTER 11

Pieces

BY MICHAEL AND STORMIE OMARTIAN

Pieces, pieces

> *I've got all the pieces of your life*

A thousand tiny fragments

> *Of every single day*

I can put them all together

> *And there'll never be another one who can*

Jerry

I dragged into the house after singing a radio commercial in Dan Dalton's studio. Susanne stood in the kitchen. She looked like she had been crying. I knew what was coming. Before I got past the living room she would cut me to shreds. I walked toward the bedroom waiting for her to start.

She took a sharp breath. I turned and saw her give a little shudder as she looked down, pressing her lips together. She remained silent for a long moment. Then, cautiously, she unclenched her lips and stammered, "I made stuffed potatoes…your favorite. Do you want some?…Jarret's spending the night…with Brett."

Our eyes met for an instant. Although I wasn't the least bit hungry (cocaine dulls your appetite) I blurted, "Yes. I mean…okay."

I had to eat, for her sake. She was trying so hard to be nice to me. I wasn't going to ignore her efforts. I was lonely too.

Susanne put the plates on the placemats and we sat next to each other, feeling awkward. I had to force the food down — I couldn't taste anything and my stomach was in knots.

We didn't even talk. Yet somehow it seemed okay. Just eating together was a start.

I dismissed the thought of going out after that. It felt right just to sit on the couch and watch TV. Susanne washed the dishes then sat beside me. There was a gap between us but at least she was near.

Two hours passed as we watched sit-coms on TV.

Yet, during those shows, more passed than time. The blunt anger and confusion that had raged between us melted. As we sat there, daring to be together again, it slowly melted.

Eventually Susanne straightened in her seat. Her fingers rested lightly on my arm.

"Guess I'll call it a night," she said.

Her touch startled me. We'd hadn't touched in so long my senses quickened.

I gently caught her hand when she rose. She turned back and sat down again. This time, right by my side. I tenderly took her in my arms. Gradually the bitterness and pain faded as we loved each other with a sweet intensity not felt for many years.

After that night I told her, "Honey, I think I will get through this — if I know I can come home to you and your love."

Our son Jarret came home from school at the beginning of 4th grade with a note from the school nurse. It said she suspected poor vision in one eye and she thought we should have it checked.

I watched the ophthalmologist cover Jarret's left eye. He read the chart fine. But when the right eye was covered, the left eye wandered erratically. The doctor pulled a phoropter in front of Jarret and scanned his visual capabilities.

"His vision is 20/80," the doctor diagnosed. "That means what a person normally sees at 80 feet, Jarret would not see till he got as close as 20 feet. His left eye is not doing its job. It's a condition called amblyopia strabismus, or "lazy eye." We usually try to catch this much sooner, because children are visually developed by age seven. Jarret is 10. Surgery can help align the lazy eye. If it's not done, the left eye will wander, noticeably."

Walking out together, I pushed open the double glass doors of the office building. Jarret took advantage of my closeness.

"Dad, God's gonna heal me," he whispered.

I stared at Jarret, dumbfounded. And, in the next instant, another Presence joined us. He spoke to my heart, "When your vision is healed, Jarret's vision will be healed."

The next day I set up an appointment to get a second opinion.

"His vision is 20/60," the second ophthalmologist told us two weeks later.

"See Dad! God's healing me already," Jarret said openly. I smiled weakly. I was once so bold. Now I felt embarrassed as the doctor self-consciously brushed a speck of lint off his white lab coat.

"I need to tell you, Mr. McClain," the doctor added, "that surgery will only fix Jarret's eyes cosmetically. There's no guarantee his left eye will ever work properly."

That night, our family gathered in Jarret's room. He was on the edge of his top bunk with the furry snout of our reddish Cocker Spaniel, Radar, beside him.

Susanne sat beneath on the bottom bunk and I sat across in a chair by Jarret's youth desk.

Since Susanne's forgiveness, we'd begun to have these family devotions. Often, during the nightly ritual, emotions choked me. I was reminded of summer nights at my grandparents' house. Pap would pick a verse and, in his confident, southern Texas drawl, read aloud. As if on cue, we each followed the reading with something we were thankful for. That was Mem and Pap's idea of faith: read the Bible, apply it to your life, and be thankful.

"Let's see." I tried to look at ease. "Tonight we're at Luke 11:33-36."

I began. "'No one lights a lamp and hides it. Instead, he puts it on a lampstand to give light to all who enter the room. Your eyes…'" I looked up at Jarret, then tried to find my place again.

"'Your eyes will light up your inward being. A pure eye,'" I could hardly believe what I was reading, "'lets sunshine into your soul. A lustful eye shuts out the light and plunges you into darkness.'"

The words held meaning Jarret knew nothing about. Again God was speaking to me about my spiritual vision. I cleared my throat, and continued slowly. "So watch out that the sunshine isn't blotted out. If you are filled with light within, with no dark corners, then your face will be radiant too, as though a floodlight is beamed upon you"(LB).

"Isn't that neat, Dad?" Jarret asked. "Just like I told you, God knows about my eyes and He's gonna heal them."

I could only nod. Another voice was calling me. I could practically see Pap's face — anxious, concerned. "Be Sunshine again," he pleaded.

While Jarret heard hope for healing in that scripture, I heard a challenge. Would I continue lusting after the high I found in cocaine…and remain in darkness? Or would I push it aside, as tantalizing as it was, and choose to shine my light once again?

Looking at the faces of my tired wife and hopeful little son, the powerful lure of more glamorous company pulled at me. Why couldn't I do a little of both? Be here for my family and be out with the crowd? I was hip there — no dishes or bills or bad days. Just laughs and pats on the back.

The next day I decided to call Dr. Rosenbaum at the UCLA Jules Stein Eye Institute. I'd go to the top and settle this thing once and for all — Jerry McClain style. Nothing in my life had to change. We just needed a pro to tell us what needed to be done and we'd get Jarret fixed up right away.

"I'm sorry," the receptionist said. "We're booked for months."

She didn't know who she was talking to. Sweetly, but firmly, I told her I would come and sit in her waiting room day after day until we were seen. She squeezed us in.

Seated before Dr. Rosenbaum, my confidence drained with each word he spoke. "There's been muscle damage — right here." He pointed his pen to a model of an eyeball. "If we don't do something, he's likely to lose the vision in his left eye. The brain shuts down the controls when one eye won't cooperate. The stronger eye does the work for both. Surgery will shorten the muscle on the left eye and, regardless of how well it is or isn't working, at least it will look normal." My gaze flitted around the shrinking room.

"There is something you can do, though, that might mean the difference between his wearing thick glasses or normal glasses after the surgery."

I looked up.

"It'll take both of you working together."

He reached for a stand and some charts. "Three times a day I want you to look at these charts, Jarret," the doctor instructed. "See, this set has bars on it. This one has green bars. Your job, Dad, is to gradually move the charts further apart, as long as Jarret can always bring the two images together. We're going to give that weak eye a good work-out. Keep track of his progress. He'll need you rooting for him or he'll get discouraged."

He turned back to Jarret and winked. "Your brain's going into spring training, slugger."

There was hope then. But it all hinged on one requirement: we work together.

My son needs me.

In that instant I saw the ugliness of my past selfishness. Jarret needs me now. But what about the hundreds of times he needed me before and I wasn't there? When he went to bed most nights — it was his mom who whispered stories until his tired eyes flickered shut. And when he woke, fresh for a new day, I was so hung over I could do little more than stagger through the kitchen.

Afternoons were a little better. Still, I often promised him, "We'll go for ice cream after school," or "Let's play ball when you come home," and then leave a note, not coming back for days.

Jarret needed me all those times, too.

And there were the things he didn't know about. I wasn't earning the money I used to, but I sure was spending it.

Susanne tried to fill the gaps — long days working, then holding us together at home. She used to go about with a song on her lips and a twinkle in her eye. Now she was practical and quiet.

Friends and relatives knew of the change, too, and kept their distance...from all of us.

Jarret jumped down from the examining table. I stood and tussled his red hair. Three times a day will be just a down payment of all I owe ya', little guy.

As if reading my thoughts, Jarret smiled up at me. A flicker twitched in my chest. Could it be that my son's innocent, cheerful faith was lighting the smoldering ashes of my own?

"How about we go to the Apple Pan and seal the deal?" I bargained with a broad grin.

"All right!" Jarret cheered.

The doctor shook my hand and gave me the charts and stand.

I stared at them as we waited in line for available stools at the Apple Pan diner. The hamburgers popped and sizzled on the steaming grill and I felt strangely glad. These charts were going to bring more together than just Jarret's vision.

CHAPTER 12

God will make a way

BY DON MOEN

God will make a way

> *Where there seems to be no way*

He works in ways we cannot see

> *He will make a way for me*

He will be my guide

> *Hold me closely to His side*

With love and strength for each new day

> *He will make a way*

> *He will make a way*

Susanne

I shivered, standing in front of the living room window, waiting and waiting to see Jerry's car pull up the driveway. I had tried to go sleep after I tucked Jarret in. I read my Bible, even called my friend Linda Sanner and asked her to pray with me. It wasn't that it was the first time that I didn't know where Jerry was or when he was coming home. But no matter how many nights it happened, it was always frightening. Linda and her husband Dick, Jerry's best friend since childhood, reassured me it was just a matter of time until Jerry would see the light.

I rubbed my eyes and noticed the pink of daybreak peeking around the houses across the street. This wasn't the light the Sanners were referring to, but apparently it was the kind Jerry would see before he came home. I turned to go get dressed for work. Jarret suddenly ran out from his room.

"Mommy! We have to pray for Daddy!" he said.

I folded into the couch and caught my breath. "Come sit beside me, honey."

Jarret began, "Dear Jesus, please keep watch on my Daddy...."

Moments later flashing lights bounced off the walls of the living room. We sprang up and rushed to the window. A policeman was opening the back door of a patrol car. Out stepped Jerry.

"Mom, look!" Jarret pointed. Jerry's car pulled into the driveway, parked, and another officer appeared, getting out of the driver's seat.

It was a peculiar scene; neither officer was upset. They simply escorted Jerry to the door and tipped their hats at me.

We all watched them drive away, then Jerry explained.

"Whew! That was a close one. Lucky they were fans. I guess I was going pretty fast, but they loosened right up when they saw who I was. Even wanted my autograph," he laughed.

Jarret and I watched him meander to the bedroom. Then I crouched down low. "Jarret, Daddy's pretty confused right now. But we know that God told you to pray for him and that's why he didn't get in a lot of trouble." Jarret nodded his head.

It was typical of Jerry to ignore God's hand of mercy. But I recognized it clearly through all the people who saw us through those hard times. They found ways to help Jarret and me without contributing to Jerry's drug addiction. My father gave me a credit card from Montgomery Ward's to use for purchasing household necessities and clothes. A Shell credit card covered gas.

Jerry's parents gave us their Honda — knowing we

couldn't afford to repair our cars. And Jerry's mom empathized with my pain over Jerry's fall probably more keenly than anyone else could. Wanting to share the burden, she told me not to worry about school clothes for Jarret. That was her department now.

A week before Christmas in 1980, when I was working for Dorothy Day Children's Theatrical Agency, I confided to Darlene Honeycut that I didn't even have an extra dime to buy Jarret a Christmas gift. Darlene adored Jarret's cheerful personality and freckled face.

At noon Christmas Eve day, I left the office party and went back to my desk to retrieve my purse. A white envelope jutted out. On it was written, "From the Elves." Inside were ten $10 bills. Years later I found out Darlene had told our friends Paul and Kathy Lee Johnson (now Kathie Lee Gifford) of my predicament. They were the elves who brought Christmas cheer to Jarret that year.

The following Christmas my sister Diane thought being with family might be the greatest gift we could receive. So, knowing of our meager means, she sent us three airline tickets to Seattle.

Several summers after, Jerry's brother Kent and his wife, Myrna, saw to it that we took a break away and joined them at their cabin on Lake Almanor in northern California. We floated on the lake in inner tubes, water skied and played volleyball. (Jarret still treasures those times as the best family vacations we ever had.)

The Omartians also tried to help us regain normalcy by inviting us over for dinner after church. And

Claudia Niesen, who set up our first blind date, called regularly, sometimes with a reason and sometimes, unabashedly, without one.

And I called her…and many others, like long-time friends Larry and Sharon Griffith. They let me vent my struggles over the phone. Min was my counselor, but night after night, after Jarret was asleep and Jerry had gone out, it helped to talk and sort out priorities.

Money for groceries was top of the list. The Lord must have tapped my phone line and then transferred the call into the dreams of Kurt and Patty Hardy. I later wrote this poem to thank them for their love gift of food:

> *Two little bags in a row*
> *Who they came from, we don't know*
> *There was no note, there was no bell*
> *Do you suppose from Heaven they fell?*
>
> *Two little bags with food galore*
> *Cookies, oranges, chicken and more…*
> *Soups and eggs and bread…ya boo!*
> *Even dog food for Radar too*
>
> *Must have been angels in the night*
> *Who knew so well our financial plight*
> *So they made a trip to the grocery store*
> *Then left the goodies at our door*
>
> *It seems when our burdens are too hard to bear*
> *He gives us friends who are willing to share*

Their money, their time, their love, their prayers
Can there be any doubt that our God really cares?

And it seems that in doing, we're always blessed
And once again you've passed the test
You saw a need and you helped out
That's what LOVE is all about

Two little bags in a row
Where they came from, we're sure we know
Two little bags filled with Love
Two little bags from Heaven above

I was spiritually nourished at Church On The Way. We'd attended since the church was founded with just 100 members and, through weekly Bible studies, we enjoyed friendship and fellowship with other Christian performers like Pat Boone, Dean Jones, Paul Johnson, Barry McGuire, Mike and Stormie Omartian, Jim and Carol Owens and the Herring family (The 2nd Chapter of Acts). During the years of bewilderment, they all rallied around me, and tears still fall whenever I'm near Annie Herring; she exudes God's love.

Besides giving us the groceries, Patty Hardy paid my way to a women's retreat put on by Church On The Way. It helped to get away and mingle. It also reminded me that my life wasn't the only one with troubles. I used to be bewildered by emotional women. I couldn't understand their distress. But that was when my life was dreamy. Now that I was living a nightmare, I sensed a new compassion for hurting hearts.

The next Sunday at church, Pastor Jack Hayford underlined the source of that compassion. He reminded us that Jesus wept with His friends. He was a man of sorrows. Everyone around me sat riveted — many marriages were on the brink of disaster. As Pastor Jack talked, though, it was as if he was talking directly to me. He challenged, "Can God put together what man put asunder?"

Once home, my faith recharged, I sat on the couch and wrote a poem to Jerry. God could bring us back together. Somehow, though, Jerry had to come to his senses. He had to see that while I still loved him, I hoped and prayed he'd turn back into the man I married.

I gave this poem to him on our wedding anniversary:

> *Fifteen years married and what have we got?*
> *By worldly standards…not a whole lot*
>
> *We own a house but it needs repairs*
> *Second-hand furniture with rips and tears*
>
> *No pool, no spa, no microwave*
> *No dishwasher that much time would save*
>
> *Our cars are failing day by day*
> *They only work because we pray*

Our bank account is worse than low
Where oh where do our paychecks go?

Extravagant spenders? Hardly the case
Just tryin' to keep up with the old rat race

No credit cards to buy us time
We're gettin' by on one thin dime

You're in and out of jobs it seems
Trying to latch onto those dreams

For years it seems we had so much
Those days of travel and songs and such

Our hearts were open and honest and true
I believed in…and worshipped…and followed you

Of late the days are not so warm
We do and say things that bring such harm

We hide our feelings deep inside
And look away to swallow our pride

Will we ever return again
To treasured times of way back when

Times that were spoiled by darkened deeds
And bad decisions from sown seeds

My heart is longing to love again
Can it happen? If so...when?

Can I put my trust in you?
Believing the things you say and do?

Will I see my Jerry Purl
Once again arise...unfurl?

This is the time...Arise! Awake!
The blessing is here for us to take

Step out and believe it can be done
The battle is over...the victory's been won

Much was given — much was taken
But not for a moment were we forsaken

His hand was strong upon our lives
But where, oh where, were our eyes?

I believe that we were meant to be
And should not live lives separately

We have no right to take the joy
Away from Jarret...our precious boy

The wilderness has been our way
But Canaan is but steps away

Together we can reach that land
Give me your heart...give me your hand

Let's begin our marriage anew
Giving Him counsel in all that we do

Renew with me our sacred vow
Begin with Him...begin again now.

CHAPTER 13

Turn, Turn, Turn

FROM THE BOOK OF ECCLESIASTICS — PETE SEEGER MUSIC

RECORDED BY PRATT & McCLAIN ON SONRISE/BENSON RECORDS

To everything turn, turn, turn

There is a season turn, turn, turn

And a time for every purpose under heaven

"Hey, Mr. McClain, I saw you on TV last night. I couldn't believe it. You were on the "Dick Clark Reunion Show." I didn't know you used to sing."

Three weeks earlier, I had started teaching geometry and algebra at Alemany High School. I felt like I was building a new life. My students filed in.

"Yeah, I saw you, too, Mr. McClain. You looked a lot different," another student jabbed. "Dick Clark said your name though, so I knew it was you."

A new life — now this. I pretended I changed careers by choice. Truth was, I resented having to teach. The salary was low and the job was...humbling. I used to be the one in the spotlight, the one reporters asked questions. In my classroom, I was just another teacher. Until today. Now I was a teacher with a curious past.

The class was abuzz with the news that I was on TV. A smile spread on Marybeth's face. "Check it out, Mr. McClain. My parents asked me to bring this in. They want your autograph." It was my album, *Happy Days*.

That night I sat by the edge of my bed and wept. How could I have thrown it all away?

When "Happy Days" was a hit, I set my sights on having our own TV show. Variety shows were the trend of the day and I felt certain we could act circles around Tony Orlando & Dawn.

After that, I hoped to jump into politics. My celebrity popularity would give me exposure, my love for law would make me a good congressman.

But I lost focus on why I was out there entertaining in the first place. I tripped on conceit and landed on my face. Now I knew I had to refocus my life — but how? Teaching 10th grade geometry was never in my dreams.

My eyes strayed to the *Living Bible* on my nightstand. I opened it randomly and read.

"Sing a new song to the Lord! Sing it everywhere...Each day tell someone that He saves" (Psalm 96:1-2 LB).

I stared at the words — amazed. "This is for me, isn't it, Lord?" I asked.

My tears crinkled the page. "You're going to give me a new song, aren't you? This time, though," I promised, "I'm totally sold out to You."

I went to sleep that night with the words running through my head. "...Each day tell someone that He saves."

The next morning there was a notice in my school mailbox. Faculty members were needed to monitor parking at the junior varsity football games. Instantly, I knew what the Lord wanted me to do.

I stepped into the athletic director's office and spoke with Dudley Rooney.

"You don't have to look for anyone else to supervise the parking. I volunteer to do it the entire season. I'll come at 4:30, direct the parking for the junior varsity game, then stay and help with the parking for the varsity game."

It was a small beginning, but I was finally catching on to the program: I had to be humbled to be healed.

The following March, after church, I sat in the car of a hero of mine, Terry Debay, and found out what else God had in store for me.

Terry played football for UCLA in the '50s. In fact, when I was 11, I watched him play the day I almost ran away from home. I thought my disappearance might bring my divorced parents back together. Then the phone rang. It was a friend from church, reminding me we were going to see UCLA beat USC. I grabbed my jacket and was out the door. I forgot all about running away.

Now, 30 years later, Terry was trying to help me deal with the dark clouds that engulfed my life.

"I'm not afraid of failure," I told Terry. "It's just so hard to live with."

After the diagnosis of Jarret's condition, I continued to do drugs — in studios, during a chance meeting with old friends. And every time I went back to drugs,

Jarret's progress wavered.

Then, on January 10, I finally quit taking drugs, cold turkey. I was at a coke party, with plenty available, when I remembered I had a poem in my wallet that my father wrote. Looking for comfort, I slipped it out and walked to a secluded corner as I read:

> *I remember, I remember*
> > *the house where I was born*
> *The little window where the sun*
> > *came peeping in at morn.*
> *He never came a wink too soon,*
> > *nor brought too long a day*
> *But now I often wish the night*
> > *had borne my breath away*
> *I remember, I remember*
> > *the fir trees dark and high*
> *I used to think their slender tops*
> > *were close against the sky*
> *It was a childish ignorance*
> > *but now 'tis little joy*
> *To know I'm farther off from heaven*
> > *than when I was a boy.*

My dad was a closet alcoholic. He died at 49.

Instead of comfort, it was a message from the grave, a message from one left behind. When his dream derailed, he gave up trying to get back on track. Would I do the same?

My wallet lay open. Jarret's school picture stared up at me.

I shook my head. What was I doing sitting among the dying when two precious people were praying for me to live? I looked around me. I was in a crowd of lonely people, driven by self-centeredness — thinking only of their next pleasurable high. They didn't care for me. I guess I didn't care very deeply for them either. But back home were two willing to love me even when I didn't return love. It was *their* company I needed to be in.

I left right away.

But the craving didn't. The jitters, the shakes, the withdrawal from prescription drugs — I went through it all. My heart raced so fast at times I imagined my head would burst from the pressure.

Now I had to face the mess I made of our lives without a high to escape to.

Terry listened to my story, then told me his. He, too, faced tough obstacles.

He had started out on the right track. He was a professing Christian and took part in Bill Bright's Campus Life meetings. After football, Terry went on to have a successful real estate business and started a family.

"Jerry, I nearly lost it all to the bottle," he said. "But I got a second chance. I found the cure for the mess I was in. It's the Holy Spirit's power. It will get you back on track, Jerry. God will give it to you, if you just ask."

I stared at the dust on the dashboard.

Terry continued, "Paul described the Holy Spirit like a deposit on the inheritance we'll get someday in heaven."

I certainly needed a little bit of heaven.

Terry put his hand on my shoulder and prayed for God to take over. "Lord, You know Jerry better than anybody. And You love him far more than anyone. He needs Your help now, Lord. He needs to feel close to You. Lead him as he attempts to make things right with his family. Help him become a strong leader for You once again.

"And now I ask you to baptize Jerry in the Holy Spirit and give him a language of prayer."

A lightness trickled down on me. Weariness lifted.

With eyes still closed, I raised my head to thank God for His presence. Instead, a flow of words came out — not English, not gibberish either. A real language — just one I couldn't understand.

It was marvelous; my tongue was loosened with a freedom to tell God how grateful I was. I felt transported: I wasn't in a car, I was in heaven. I didn't want it to stop.

But then I opened my eyes and saw a group of people walking by. I remembered that Susanne was waiting for me and Terry's wife would probably want to get their family home for dinner. Still, I was relieved of the burden.

I smiled into the brightness of the sun.

When I was taking drugs I took for granted God's protective hand. But now my eyes were opened. In my mind I relived the many shady places I had gone. Guardian angels must have been looking out for me — big time.

But was the danger all in the past? I owed several drug dealers thousands of dollars, and they and others were always bugging me for fresh leads. It wouldn't be long until they'd come knocking on my door. I'd heard of guys killed for owing them just $50.

Then I thought of a ceremony that I'd taken part in at church. Maybe it would be a way of protecting our home. Church on the Way had recently dedicated a new building by circling the perimeter and anointing the inside walls. How great it would be if, once I came home, I felt safe spiritually as well as physically.

No one was home, so I found a jar of oil under the sink and walked outside to the back yard and around to the front, sprinkling the oil in front of me. I prayed for God to guard us against the enemy and any drug users who might come to bother us. Then I walked in through the front door, sprinkling oil on the door frames and dabbing the walls, praying God's blessings on Susanne and Jarret.

That was it. I didn't think of it again until years later when I saw one of the drug dealers I owed money. Standing outside a car wash, I recognized Mongo. He's hard to miss. He's Hawaiian, stands 5'8" but weighs about 350 pounds. He remembered me only half as well. It looked like he was still part of the fast lifestyle.

I told him how I'd been convicted by God and quit drugs, then asked, "I've always wondered, though, why you never came after me. I owed you a lot of money."

He looked at me as if my drug use had made me dumb.

"I *did* come to your house," he said emphatically. "I was coming to get the money or get you. But when I walked up your driveway, there was a old man sitting in a chair on your front porch. He said, 'Mongo, you must go away and not return.' I don't do all that psychic stuff. But this old cat made me feel weird. So I figured, I didn't know what you'd gotten into, but that voodoo stuff was worth any amount of money, so I left."

Two weeks later, I ran into Mark, another guy I used to buy drugs from — and owed a lot of money. I told him of my years free from drugs and why I'd changed. He too shook his head when I asked him why he hadn't come after me. "But I *did* come to your house. It's just that…man, it was a trip. Your old gardener knew my name somehow and told me never to return. He said your house was a house of God. He had this look in his eyes that…well, he freaked me out. So I just split, man. Forget about it."

I don't know any old men who sit on my porch and tell people to go away, and I don't have an old gardener. God does answer prayer, though. I just didn't know He had done it. Our concern at that time was with Jarret's eyes.

The surgery to fix Jarret's "lazy eye" on July 25, 1986 took four long hours. Susanne and I tried to read the magazines and newspapers in the hospital waiting room, but it was hard to concentrate. Just as I glanced at the latest baseball scores, a sudden warmth came over me. Susanne looked over at me and asked if I was okay. I touched my cheeks; they were hot. The sensation diminished gradually, but I suspected it left a lasting value. It seemed a reminder of God's presence there with us — but there was more. Something within me felt changed.

After the surgery, we met Dr. Rosenbaum in the hall. "It looks like a success," he told us, snapping off his gloves. I hugged Susanne. He added, "We need to test the eye again in a month."

Those first few days following the surgery, the bandage patched over Jarret's eye needed to be changed routinely. As I applied clean gauze I reminded him, "A pure eye lets sunshine into the soul." That was the scripture we had read together nine months earlier. Since then, we had faithfully increased the difficulty of his eye exercises. Only time would tell if it paid off.

As we wondered about the condition of Jarret's eye, I was encouraged by the improved condition of my spiritual eyes. They had gotten a correlating work-out. Coming home every day, loving my wife and son in a thousand practical ways — that, I was discovering, was the focused vision of a man after God's heart. Like David after his confession of sin with Bathsheba, I felt back in God's graces. Perhaps if Pap were around he'd even call me "Sunshine" again.

A month later, when we arrived at Dr. Rosenbaum's office, several doctors were talking with him. They said it would take a few minutes to do Jarret's testing. Meanwhile, they tried to prepare us for the worst.

"The eye muscles appear to be holding very well. But remember, that doesn't mean the problem's totally corrected. Jarret will probably still need to wear glasses to see well, possibly prism glasses," Dr. Rosenbaum said. The other doctors nodded in agreement.

Then, oddly, Dr. Rosenbaum kept repeating tests. Susanne and I looked at each other. Again and again, he changed the lenses on the instrument and asked Jarret, "Can you read the last line?"

Finally, Dr. Rosenbaum swung the phoropter aside. "This has never happened before." He took a long look at Jarret before he continued.

"You have 20/20 vision. You don't even need glasses."

CHAPTER 14

Me and Jesus

BY TOM T. HALL

RECORDED BY JERRY McCLAIN ON COLUMBIA RECORDS

Me and Jesus, got our own thing goin'

Me and Jesus, got it all worked out

Me and Jesus, got our own thing goin'

Don't need anybody to tell us what it's all about

Even before Jerry turned his life back around, I was
free. I'd thrown off the pressing need that once pos-
sessed me to scrutinize Jerry's every move. Like those
days following my prayer of commitment with Jan
Lindsey years ago, I was in love with the Lord again.
And knowing I was loved by God made loving Jerry
easier.

"Me and Jesus, we got our own thing going," I'd
sing around the house. It was the song Jerry recorded
with Michael Omartian and the 2nd Chapter of Acts ten
years earlier. The chorus set to motion the thrill in my
heart. "…Me and Jesus, we got it all worked out…."

Wanting to please Jesus — that was my guidepost.
Everything fell in line behind Him. I was kind because I
knew He wanted me to be. I was just, fair with my
words at home, because Jerry wasn't my Lord, Jesus
was. That "thing going" was as real as the beating of my
heart — and as constant.

My friends at work even noticed it. I began working at Village Christian School in 1981. Besides being a
haven for me emotionally, it was also a haven for me
artistically. I taught 1,000 kids in kindergarten through
sixth grade. It was quite a challenge, but I gloried in it.
To help the school celebrate holidays, I wrote Christmas and Easter musicals, taught them to all my classes

and, in no time, we were bringing the house down. It was just like being on stage again. Linda Minkler, who befriended me at Village, became my writing partner — we were the Rodgers and Hammerstein of the school.

Jarret attended school with me. I arranged it so I could keep a close eye on him. Or so I thought. Instead, God used it to show me how He'd protected Jarret through all of Jerry's dark nights. He was such a carefree kid — happy just to breathe the air, just to tell another corny joke. He'd swing his arms around me and say, "Mom, I love you," just when I needed it. Although I gave him a hard time about picking up his room and practicing his piano lessons, I loved him through and through. During those dark years, Jarret was the contrast of normalcy in our nightmare. Hidden under God's wing of protection, he came out unscathed.

And traveling to and from school with Jarret made me realize I wasn't the only one with a song in my heart. But Jarret's had never left. "What a friend we have in Jesus," he sang along with me at church and in our car on the way to school.

"It's that Friend who saved us," I wanted to tell him. "Not just from Satan. He saved us from hell on earth. You and me, son, we're walking on air blown by the Holy Spirit. You don't want to know how hurt and bitter you might have become if Jesus wasn't your buffer."

Jerry, too, noticed our son's rightness. Often, during family devotions, Jerry stared in amazement when

Jarret applied the scripture reading to his life.

"Ya' know, I think I ought to forgive that guy," he said after being treated rudely that day. Our scripture reading was about loving our neighbors. "He might be a jerk, but I guess I need to just let it go."

Let it go. As Min told me, it was the key to a better life. A life where Satan didn't have a stronghold, but Jesus did.

As a family, we had to let many things go to rebuild our lives. We had declared bankruptcy and went through the humiliating experience of having our cars repossessed. I bit my lips hard, trying not to berate Jerry, when the truck backed up in the early morning, waking the neighbors and loading the vehicles.

If they hadn't heard our fighting, they now got the picture of our financial plight.

I tried to face it bravely. Why be ashamed? Everyone makes mistakes. Still, I swallowed hard on that one.

But the comfort of Jesus' presence back in our home really did overshadow the consequences we had to live with.

"I've got it!" I said as we looked at the bills. "We'll have a garage sale." A light dawned on Jerry and Jarret's faces. We were behind two months on our mortgage payment and it was due in one week. I walked around the house picking up things. "We can sell this platter, and this statue. This antique glass vase might bring $10." I stopped. "What we really need, though, are big-ticket items."

"I'll sell my Legos," Jarret piped up.

My heart ached. Jarret loved his Legos.

"Oh, honey. I guess you're right. We should all give up something that's important to us — kind of make a sacrificial offering to help the cause."

"Guess the VCR will have to go then." Jerry was serious and I couldn't believe it. In his darkest moods, he stroked his pride by watching videos of our past shows, brooding over what he'd lost professionally.

But the VCR was a big-ticket item (plus I'd be glad to have the brooding go).

"What about this, Mom?" Jarret pointed to Jerry's old guitar.

"We'll save the precious stuff, Jarret. Just sell what we can do without. You never know when that guitar might come in handy."

"Maybe I'll play that guitar one day, Mom."

"Maybe. Let's see…." I opened the kitchen cupboard and saw Mem's scorch-it-till-it's-burned frying pan. Memories rushed up to meet me. Hugs, laughter, a joke going on and on — Pap, Mem and Jerry and I all adding to it. With the faces of Pap and Mem in my mind, I hugged the black, solid pan, filled with assurance. We will have good times again.

"Hey, maybe we need a hook to make this sale really successful." Jerry had his producer hat on again. "We could make it an experience they'll never forget."

"I can make posters," Jarret offered.

"I can sing like Elvis, put on a little performance."

I put my hand up. "Hopefully, you'll be too busy

collecting cash to gyrate."

"Susanne, everybody's into Elvis these days. It's a selling point."

"True. But let's keep it toned down, okay?"

On the day of the sale, I passed the orange couch the boys had hauled out. A big sign was taped on it. "Elvis slept here."

I found a piece of paper and folded a sign for the ashtray on the nightstand beside it. I wrote, "Elvis put his cigarette butts here."

Pretty soon there were Elvis signs everywhere. And Jerry was right, garage sale shoppers loved it. We rang bells, gave away door prizes and practically jumped through hoops to make a sale. And we shed a private tear or two when our prized possessions walked away.

In the end we made $1,600. We needed $1,500 for mortgage payments. Grateful for God's provision, we stuck $50 in an envelope for the church offering and took ourselves out for a celebration dinner.

We'd succeeded, with God's help.

Jerry succeeded in his teaching job, too. He was unlike any other geometry teacher at Alemany High School. The nuns twittered at his one liners in the staff lunch room. And the students loved him. His stories provided an occasional breather from angles and degrees. His light-hearted banter let them know he saw each one of them as individuals.

Kids often wrote him notes, telling how he had affected them.

"You're the best teacher I ever had!"

"Last night at a party my friend passed me a joint. I didn't smoke it because I remembered what you said about drugs messing up your life."

I just shook my head when he showed me notes like that. What a wonderful blessing to come from such a difficult time.

Jarret received fine schooling, since we received a teacher's discount on his tuition. Once he graduated from eighth grade at Village where I taught, he transferred to Alemany High School to be with Dad.

It was a great time for Jarret. He was on the league champion cross country team, treasurer of the student body, Boy's State Rep, and he acted in and directed plays. But what was most special were the times he dropped by his dad's classroom to visit. Jerry and Jarret were a couple of pals.

Over dinner at night, I could hardly get a word in. All they talked about was what was happening at school and people they both knew (and I didn't).

Really, I was glad it was that way. They needed to make up for the lost years, make every minute count. And Jarret carried on several traditions of his father. He learned to play Jerry's guitar and, with his close friend Chris, Michael Omartian's son, he was part of the youth worship team at church.

When Jarret left for Pepperdine University in Malibu, California, I knew we would miss him terribly, but we were excited for him. (Of course, we hardly had a chance to miss him — he was back the next weekend with dirty laundry.) His high school years had been a time of real closeness for our family. If I wasn't able to go to a track meet or a play rehearsal, I didn't worry. Jerry was always there, cheering him on. So Jarret left with our blessings, knowing that in our hearts we were an inseparable trio.

Because I chose to forgive Jerry when I was suffocating from hurt and anger, God rescued me and now I have a son and a husband I'm proud of.

CHAPTER 15

Happy days

BY CHARLES FOX AND NORMAN GIMBEL

RECORDED BY PRATT & McCLAIN ON WARNER BROS. RECORDS

Sunday, Monday, Happy Days

Tuesday, Wednesday, Happy Days

Thursday, Friday, Happy Days

Saturday, What a day

Rockin' all week with you.

These Happy Days are yours and mine

These Happy Days are yours and mine

Happy Days.

I had been out of the entertainment industry, teaching at Alemany High School for six years when I got a call from Bob Cotterell of Sonrise Music Co. He was putting together a collection of early Jesus Movement music and heard I could help him get clearance for several old songs by Michael Omartian.

I was glad to help since I owned the masters. As Bob and I worked together we hit it off. He was impressed by my knowledge of the music industry and asked me to co-produce the triple discs "The Rock Revival/Original Music from the Jesus Movement."

A rush of emotions came back — like getting behind the wheel of my old, red, 1964 convertible. I'd always loved the business side of entertainment, and "The Rock Revivals" stirred that up again.

Promoting the CDs turned into a full-time job and I began to wonder if I should quit teaching high school. Cautiously, and somewhat hopefully, I thought maybe this was God's way of giving me a small niche back in the music world.

As I struggled with the issue, I received a notice that "Happy Days" was being re-released on several compilations. I couldn't believe it. A comeback?

Apparently so. And it snowballed into a big one. Report after report arrived: "Happy Days" was suddenly selling like "crazy" again as part of *Time-Life Greatest Hits, Memory-Time Europe, Rhino Records Super Hits of the '70s* and *TV's Greatest Hits.*

Even more amazing, Nickelodeon Cable Network announced their plans to run the sitcom "Happy Days" nightly in prime time. In addition, "Nick at Night" joined forces with Simon & Schuster for a line of books and specialty merchandise to introduce a whole new generation to The Fonz and Richie Cunningham.

Faced with these new developments, I was assailed by conflicting feelings: excitement, anticipation, confusion, remorse. My mind wandered back to that appearance years ago on "American Bandstand" when Dick Clark asked me about Las Vegas. I winced as I recalled how I let God and His message down: instead of allowing my light to shine, I lied and said we gambled, trying to look cool.

Yet God had done so much with my life since then — my marriage was restored, my son was well and happy, my own life was full and productive. Was God now offering me a chance to redeem myself in the music business — use those gifts and talents He gave me long ago, this time for His glory, not mine?

I didn't want my pride and ambition to get in His way, so I continued to look to God for confirmation.

On the morning of February 2, 1995, I was sitting at my desk at school thinking over the past and pondering the future. Beside me was a bag full of cards and letters I'd received over the years from my high school students. They wrote me about their romantic heartbreaks, troubles at home, how they appreciated my faith in them and in God. It seemed I had made a difference in their lives, that God had blessed my teaching career — just as He had my early music career. But was I to continue teaching, or not?

Groping for guidance, I picked up a devotional booklet I kept on my desk. "Lord, please speak to me. Should I quit teaching?" I prayed. Then I opened to the narrative for that day.

It said,

> "I was rummaging through some old files the other day, when I ran across a big envelope of treasures, a collection of thankyou notes from the last year I taught high school…."

What an uncanny "coincidence." Just when I was asking God if I should quit my teaching job I read "the last year I taught high school." Surely it was no coincidence: God heard my prayer and answered me directly. I immediately walked to the principal's office and told him what happened: it would be my last year of teaching. God had a new plan for Jerry McClain.

As I related the story to Susanne later I was still amazed at the wonder of God — His grace, His mercy, His intervention in our lives.

The next Wednesday, I got up at five in the morning to fit in a work-out before school. As I got on my

exercise bike I noticed the same devotional booklet
that had triggered my resignation.

"Hey, it's my birthday. Maybe I'll hit another 'home
run.'"

I opened to February 10 and read,

"As I walked out of the chapel after a memo-
rial service for a Christian friend, the funeral
home director remarked, 'You know, there's
a big difference between the funerals of
those who are Christians and those who are
unsaved....'"

I set the booklet aside. That doesn't have anything
to do with me, I thought.

On the way to school I chastised myself. I should
have known better than to pigeon-hole God. That devotional booklet wasn't my own little magic line of com-
munication to God. He would speak to me in His own
time and in His own way. I was to remain open and
ready.

During home room period, the class and I joined
with the student's voice coming over the loudspeaker
as we saluted the American flag. Then we bowed our
heads, anticipating the usual prayer. However, our principal, Father Milbauer, interrupted with the news that
one of our seniors had died in the hospital that morning. Several students in my class gasped and two girls
collapsed into their seats.

I lifted my hands in the air, suddenly knowing how
important that reading really was. "How could I have
ever doubted you, Lord?" I said aloud.

I turned to my classroom, now filled with stunned students, and told them how I had treasured last week's reading and had dismissed the one for that day. But God did choose to speak to me again — and it was again through that booklet, even though I didn't understand it at the time.

"Like I read this morning, there is a difference between the deaths of those who are Christians and those who are not. And if you're not sure today where you would end up, I have a message for you."

As I had done with Lou Warfield long ago by the side of the Seattle hotel pool, I used the Four Spiritual Laws to tell those teenagers about God's love and salvation. Then I prayed with them before the bell rang. I also gave the same message to all five of my classes that day.

Yet I wasn't quite prepared for what happened the next day. Fourteen of those students sent me letters saying that, as a result of my talk and prayer the day before, they received Jesus as their Lord.

I sat at my desk stunned, reading their letters again and again. It was suddenly so clear.

Since the beginning, Susanne and I were destined to be together. She brought her experiences of performing with her twin sister and I brought mine that started when I sang for my father, a radio preacher. Then the fateful Spring Sing intertwined our paths until they narrowed to one. Hand in hand, we walked down a dream-like lane, entertaining and evangelizing, until I let go of our commitment to walk with God.

The brief highs could never compensate for all the misery they caused.

And fame held little significance without the love and respect of my family and friends.

But God didn't give up on me. He let down a rope for me to grab onto. I couldn't understand how Susanne was able to forgive me when I was most unforgivable. But that act of love offered me a way to climb back, regain my spiritual vision and, once again, be a dependable father and husband.

Susanne and I were now back on track and God was taking us down a new path. We'd go with a new understanding, though. God's will wasn't just to be a rerun of Happy Days. No matter where Susanne and I go, He wants us to sing a new song, a song of hope — hope for those who failed and are trying to find their way back, hope for a redeemed and fulfilled life. Maybe then we can help happy days come again to many other homes like they have to ours since Jarret's little boy prayer was answered.

"Lord," he used to pray, "please bring Daddy home so Mommy won't cry anymore."

if HAPPY DAYS

and Dark Nights has blessed you...

we'd love to hear about it!

WRITE:
Jerry and Susanne McClain
Happy Days Family Ministries
Universal Studios Station
P.O. Box 8902
Universal City, CA 91618

FOR BOOKING INFORMATION CALL:
1-818-769-2842
FAX 1-818-769-6030

Other Books From
WESTERN FRONT LTD.